Food Truck Business Plan

Handbook to Help Food Truck Event Planners or Beginners to Manage Food Trucks. Strategies of Interior Décor, Food Choices, Social Media Marketing, and Financial Planning.

Roddie L.Miller

Table of Contents

Conclusion

Introduction

Welcome to the food truck business! In this book, you will discover the many paths to creating a successful food truck operation. Our goal is to give you specific knowledge to embark on your food truck journey with confidence. The following chapters cover the many considerations involved in running a food truck as a sustainable operation and the various commitments you will need to make.

The opening chapters investigate options for organizing your funding and present some of the critical decisions you must make as you build your business plan. These include choosing an existing food truck operation, constructing your own, or partnering with a current restaurant. This book will also provide you with a roadmap for turning your creative ideas for a food truck into an actionable plan through effective design and marketing techniques. But there is so much more involved in realizing your concept for a food truck.

An entire chapter of this book is devoted to sales strategies, investigating the current options available to small business owners. These include affordable software applications for processing credit charges, handling booking arrangements, and existing in digital space where reviews are a visible part of your business and have an outsized impact. Yet another chapter walks through the many financial considerations of owning a food truck, particularly in those first critical years. You will need to consider a payment plan that works for you without creating a debt sinkhole from which it becomes impossible to escape. All this may sound intimidating, but do not worry! These are the pitfalls we will investigate together so you can be alert and avoid stumbling into them.

Of course, to get your truck up and running, you will need to know how to organize and maintain healthy operations standards and oversight on a day-to-day basis. With a small business especially, hiring and management are crucial contributors to the success or failure of your venture. In this book, we cover staffing and wage considerations and how to build trust in your relationships with your suppliers. In addition to these daily operations, you will need to consider how to approach training your staff and yourself to engage in food preparation and storage appropriately, operate business vehicles, and provide excellent customer service.

What about the truck itself? We have that covered! Together, we will help you construct a food truck that matches the unique demands of your business, including the necessary components, options for industrial suppliers, and maintenance considerations. This process ranges from choosing between an inclusive truck or a trailer to the best value grill or refrigerator for the unique demands of your selected menu. We will also help you weigh the benefits of acquiring new elements against refurbished ones.

One of the most significant and potentially overwhelming concerns for any small business is your liability. You want to know you are protecting yourself, your employees, and your customers, as well as any investors or your private capital investments. The legal aspects of food truck business ownership and operation vary by state and country, but this book will equip you with the requisite tools for approaching these considerations with confidence. We discuss taxes, relevant law, and insurance considerations, as well as the importance of remaining aware of new or changing legislation pertinent to your location.

We did not forget the customer-facing side of the foodservice industry, either. This book devotes an entire chapter to crafting a consistent and appealing menu to not only draw in business but build customer loyalty. This process involves developing a set menu of your most popular items following focus testing before expanding your offerings to include holiday and seasonal products or special deals for repeat customers.

As part of your menu offerings, it is essential to establish a solid and consistent brand that your customers, and potential customers, associate with your business. Your brand differentiates you from the competition, expanding awareness of your business. We will discuss the significance of knowing your neighborhood and the potential for partnering with other companies or local restaurants to offer promotions. Eventually, you can even consider offering branded products based on your accumulated knowledge of your customer base. Even such a seemingly simple task as planning your route can be a minefield, one we are happy to help you navigate. This book provides an overview of well-known food festivals and other food truck events, factoring in travel costs and considerations and how to build a reliable network as a food truck operator.

We are confident that you will build your food truck into a success using these tools, but what happens next? That is up to you. We will help you consider your options for selling your business for a profit, expanding your operation to include more trucks in more locations, whether an appraisal is necessary, and the platforms and connections you can leverage when considering these next steps.

As with any viable product, it is crucial to pay close attention to the numbers and act accordingly. This book offers various approaches to analyzing your customer and sales data and creating realistic projections to help you develop achievable goals. The final chapters also cover resources and membership organizations for food truck business owners. But more than this, we gathered case studies of successful food truck endeavors to give you a sense of the world you are about to step into and the possibilities that exist for those with the resilience to push past obstacles and realize their food truck dreams. We hope you are as inspired as we are by these stories of real people figuring it out and sharing their hard-earned insights to give you the best chance of success.

Now that you know what to expect, we will not keep you waiting. Together, we will equip you to face all the challenges and joys of running your food truck successfully, knowing what to expect, and prepared to confront the unexpected. We want to give your business the best possible chance to thrive and give you the support you need to make this happen. We know you are eager to begin building your food truck business and get those wheels on the road. Let's get started!

Chapter 1: Getting Started

Setting Goals

The odds are good that you have been thinking about starting a food truck business for some time. Maybe it started when you bit into an astonishingly tasty food truck burrito and realized you could serve almost any food out of a truck, or when you had a sudden inspiration of a name for the truck that would match its dessert burritos even better. Perhaps you have already begun to piece together some long-term objectives, specific goals that you want to accomplish with your food truck. You might already own a restaurant and are looking to expand. But if you have not had time to consider the features of your truck, don't worry. Now is the time to set those goals and make a step-by-step plan you can follow to achieve them. This book will walk you through establishing smart, achievable goals and give you the informational tools to make them happen.

At this point, your food truck business plan does not need to be set in stone. In fact, it should be flexible to account for all the unknowns that will alter your original timeline. However, it is important to have your goals in writing because they give you a good perspective on where you are on your business-building journey and, during those times when you may get discouraged, are evidence of how far you have already come. Each step of your plan will be carefully worked out through each chapter of this book. By the end of this initial chapter, you should have the beginnings of a solid business plan and can begin putting your food truck dreams into practice.

For now, all you need is a single goal that the rest of your business plan will help you work toward, sometimes called a mission statement. This final goal will likely be something along the lines of "owning and operating a profitable food truck in my hometown" or "making a $200,000 profit from a food truck over the next two years" or even simply "owning three smoothie food trucks". Whatever you choose, you should craft a goal that matches what you want to get out of this endeavor.

Food trucks can be incredibly lucrative. On average, established food trucks generate between $200,000 and $550,000 in revenue each year. Of course, food trucks also come with high startup costs, usually around $50,000, and come with significant maintenance and operational costs. You can expect your profit margin—which refers to the amount of profit you as an owner receive from each sale as a percentage of a dollar—at between 7% and 8% on average. Generally speaking, this means that your food truck business will rely on a high volume of sales to generate significant profits. One of our goals in this book is to help you understand how best to capitalize on your food truck's mobility to maximize these sales.

As is clear in these figures, the initial startup investment for a food truck business is significant, perhaps even more than you were expecting. Give yourself some time to adjust to the idea while you get your long-term goal in writing. It is also important that you understand this startup money need not come out of your own pocket. There are many methods of financing your food truck, which we will investigate at length, but for now, it is important to have a clearly articulated goal for your business.

Now that you have established that long-term goal, it will be easier to establish the steps between there and where you are now. When you are making any kind of business plan, you will need to consider every aspect of your business. That is what this book is here to help with. Throughout the following chapters, we will consider everything from financial stability to the creative facets of your food truck business. For now, we recommend breaking down these bigger hurdles into smaller, achievable goals. As you work through this book, make notes for yourself. When you are prompted to consider various options for names, for instance, take the time to brainstorm and make notes of your favorite names before running them through focus testing, or at least making certain your partner or best friend approves. This book will walk you through all the details of developing a comprehensive business plan for your food truck and, as we do, keep your timeline in the back of your mind.

For example, use your notes to create an ideal timeline for when you want to accomplish each piece of the puzzle that will eventually become your business. If you want to have all your permits approved by a certain date, research how long it might take for your submissions to be processed and back up your goal submission date to account for that extra time. Give yourself some wiggle room, too. Especially with a new business, there are always new things popping up that require your immediate attention, so make a timeline that is ambitious but reasonably so. You do not want to burn out, especially not before you have even begun!

Defining Your Business

Now that you have your final goal, it is time to consider your first foundational step to getting there. What is it? Simply put, your first step is creating a detailed definition of your food truck business that will function as your formal business plan. This is sometimes called an executive summary. However, it may not seem immediately obvious as to why it is important to have a clearly defined description of your business until you consider that you will need it in many parts of the business-building process.

It will be useful as part of pitches to potential investors and on loan applications and permits asking you to describe your business. Having a specific description can also increase your confidence when establishing relationships with the many businesses and individuals who will need to commit to working with you before your truck even exists physically. It communicates why and how you believe your business will be successful and provides a sense of exactly what your business is, from a general overview to how it originated and future goals. For these reasons, it should be engaging and interesting to read. Let your personality show through the words. Just because this is, technically, a business document does not mean it needs to be dry or boring; just the opposite. Your food truck business idea is full of life and promise, so your description of it should be as well.

This definition is not something we expect you to generate out of thin air. Unlike your final goal, which is more straightforward, you will likely need some external guidance to help create this description. As you work through this book as a future food truck owner, you will obtain a better sense of how many considerations are involved in running a food truck. For the purposes of a business definition, you will not need to include all of them, though many of these aspects of food truck operations will inform your business description. For now, remember that your description is fluid and will function best if you are willing to edit it as you expand your knowledge of food trucks. By the end of this book, you should have a refined business description in which you have complete confidence. At that point, it should become a final document that will not undergo any major change without significant cause.

Your business description should be concise, no more than two typed pages. If possible, you should memorize it, too, so that you can easily reference details of your concept when speaking with investors. Do not expect to already be able to complete each of these sections. As we progress through the chapters, you will build a complete picture of your business and be able to articulate it in this executive summary form. Essentially, your summary will contain these key parts:

- Overview: A short explanation of the who, what, where, and why of your food truck business. This is where you introduce the name and purpose of your business.
- Products/Services: Here, you will provide information on the food you will sell. You do not need to include a full menu, just a general explanation of the types of dishes and your approach to sales, including if your truck will rely more on street sales, special events, or a combined approach.
- Financing: This will be a brief explanation of how much you will need to cover your startup costs and how you will use that money. Essentially, you will demonstrate that you have thought through what you will need to pay for, including your truck, marketing, permit, and food costs.
- Goal Statement: Here, you can explain your passion for your business, such as why you want to develop a food truck, what connection you have to the cuisine you will offer, how you are aware of the demand for your food truck, and your goals. Basically, you are answering the question: what is your ideal business? This section will be based on your final goal from the beginning of the chapter.
- Team Information: It is important to communicate how you plan to manage your business and who will be involved. People will want to feel they know you or have a good sense of who you and your team are. If you have a business partner or partner with a restaurant or other business, be sure to explain how this approach is beneficial to your food truck business.
- Projections: Potential investors will be concerned about the bottom line; namely, they will want sales projections. It is a wise idea to include in your plan a three-year model of your sales to demonstrate that you are committed to making your business a success.
- Expansion/Future Plans: Just as you began with your origin story, you will conclude your basic business plan with your vision for the future of your business. You might plan to offer new services, like catering or business

partnerships. You may plan to expand into online sales or more physical trucks, even introduce a brick-and-mortar location. Dream big but be specific and make sure you can support these plans based on your sales projections.

Each part of your plan might include several informative paragraphs, as well as bullet points and simple graphs or other graphics that effectively communicate your message. Keep your summary simple and easy to follow. This way, it will be easier for your potential investors to engage with the material. Before you show your summary to any potential investors or submit it as part of a loan application, however, run it by some people that you trust. Ideally, find someone with experience in small business ownership or investing and get their feedback. Remember, it is impossible for anyone to be an expert in everything, and even extensive internet research can only take you so far. Find people with practical experience and internalize what they can tell you. This will save you the time and effort of the trial-and-error approach.

Now that your plan is on paper make sure you know your business summary inside and out. More than anything, as you pull together all the necessary parts of your food truck, it helps to have a clear and defined picture of the end result in your mind to ensure that everything you do contributes to that end result without wasted energy spent on projects that do not fit with or support this vision. Knowing what you want your business to be will help you get there.

Once you have your business defined, get it registered! This will be particularly helpful when pursuing financing options. We will discuss the details of registration with local, state, and federal agencies in more depth in a later chapter, and the requirements vary by location. However, it is wise to get a jump start on this process since it will directly impact your ability to continue forward with the other aspects of your food truck business. For now, your local government website is a great place to start when looking for the appropriate small business registration application, as most of these sites will link to the necessary information.

Congratulations, you have officially started your food truck business! Take a moment to enjoy it. Now brace yourself because, from here on, you will need to make a lot of decisions.

Build or Buy

This is your first major business decision: whether to purchase an existing food truck business or to acquire a new or refurbished truck (with the additional option of equipment included or not) to start from scratch. But you are in luck: there is no wrong choice here. You simply need to make the best choice for your business goals. If you are more interested in making an immediate profit, it might make sense to select a food truck business that could benefit from a rebranding or relocation. If you are looking to fill a cuisine niche that has yet to be explored, it probably makes the most sense to design your own truck and begin your own brand.

Do your research. Investigate what would be required to purchase an existing business, from licensing to cost. Consider that your upfront cost is only part of what you will need to pay. Maintenance costs may be higher in an older food truck. Purchasing an existing business still gives you many options. You might buy the business itself or simply agree to operate the truck under the business owner's existing brand, arriving at an agreement that benefits both parties.

Be certain you examine how such businesses have been doing financially. These companies' annual, and sometimes even quarterly, profit statements are publicly accessible information. Once you have narrowed down your food truck businesses search to several potential options, it is worth putting in the effort to access financial records. It will give you an edge in negotiations to know exactly how much an existing business is worth, balanced against what you would be bringing to the table.

Ownership Models

Depending on your goals, it may make more sense to purchase a new or refurbished truck outright and build your own business and customer base from the ground up. This can present some slightly different risks you will need to assess. For instance, be sure of the demand for whatever product you are planning to offer. If your city is saturated with bagel shops, it might not make sense to sell bagels from your truck. This equation is complicated, however. If there are many successful bagel shops, this could mean that there is a high demand, and offering some additional benefit to the consumer with your truck could be a perfect match.

Trucks specifically offer mobility. Perhaps you could make bagels available in high-traffic locations during commuting hours. The flip side of this, of course, might be that there are few bagel shops in your city precisely because there is so little interest in bagels. Perhaps you live in a muffin mecca. Perhaps there is simply less of a breakfast food culture in your area. If this is the case, consider adapting your original plan to meet demand. Effort expended now to figure out exactly what niche your food truck fits into best will pay dividends later.

This background market research will form the foundation upon which you construct your sales approach, so be sure to do your homework! The demands of each area are different. If you have lived in the location where you plan to set up your food truck route, you probably have a good understanding of the demand for your food offerings, including location and type of cuisine. Use this knowledge but recognize that yours is only a single perspective and inherently biased. You might personally love a particular food, but religious dietary restrictions in your area might limit your market. If you are committed to your chosen food, it might also be worth considering offering alternative or substitute options to match dietary needs. All these factors will play into how you set up your truck and how much cost must be passed on to the consumer.

Also, consider the average cost of a meal in your target area, both in formal and informal restaurant settings. This will give you a window to consider. You will likely appeal to more customers by offering food at competitive prices, but you will also need to consider the cost to you of each meal. We will discuss this more in the coming chapters. For now, investigate your market.

Come up with several options that you think might appeal to consumers in your targeted area. Then perform a survey. This might be as simple as asking friends to ask their friends whether they would purchase a bagel from a food truck parked by the bus stop in the morning to something as involved as paying a market researching firm to conduct a survey for you. Look into the online reviews of similar businesses or food offerings. Find the demand and make your plan to offer the supply.

Startup Financing

There are as many ways to finance a small business as there are small business owners. You know your financial situation best, but remember that your business will likely not be profitable for the first year. When considering a business loan, look carefully at the terms of repayment and your financial projections. Do not panic about needing to create these projections; the models already exist. They are based on existing businesses and can be tailored to your business. Banks and other companies use programs to inform their investment decisions, and many of the same programs are available to you. If you prefer, consulting firms can create projections for you for a slightly higher fee.

Finding Investors

Entrepreneurs tend to speak of "angel investors" in awed tones, and you may have a connection with someone who happens to have the means and desire to commit to a large investment in your idea, but this is not how most small businesses acquire their financing. Rather, investments are often spread across several individuals or corporate sponsors. Remember to consider whether to work with an existing restaurant or business? These arrangements tend to reduce your startup costs. Either way, there will be expenses you need to cover. Do not be afraid to get creative.

While traditional lines of credit are available to registered businesses, there are some restrictions on the loans available to food truck businesses. Consider all your options before committing. Qualifying for food truck financing generally requires a minimum credit score of around 600, operating for at least six months, or meeting a revenue requirement. Unless you already own a restaurant and are expanding your offerings, this may not be an ideal approach.

Online lenders also offer lines of credit for financing specific aspects of your business, such as your equipment, the truck itself. The upside here is quick access to funds and, generally, low rates of interest. When equipping your truck, specific appliances are often eligible for this form of financing. Your truck will likely be eligible for a commercial loan at low interest. Why so low? These items themselves can be used as collateral, presenting less risk to the financer. It may also be worth leasing or leasing to buy specific pieces of equipment.

In the United States, depending on your situation, an application for a Small Business Association microloan may also be an option. However, these loans tend to require a personal guarantee. U.S.-based businesses may also be eligible for various federal loan opportunities, though these offerings and availability tend to vary year to year. In general, the Small Business Association is a great place to start with all business-related aspects of your food truck. They handle enough mobile vendors to have consolidated many resources relevant to your situation.

It is also wise to open a business credit card with a reasonable limit as an emergency measure to cover any urgent expenses that might pop up unexpectedly as you move towards your opening. Keep in mind that credit cards are subject to higher interest rates and will need to be paid off quickly. That said, they do provide a layer of security.

Crowdfunding

One resource that became available only in recent years is crowdfunding. Essentially, this involves creating an online campaign incentivizing people to contribute a small financial investment in your future business. If enough people contribute, you have your startup money. The platform may require you to pay back your investors over a period of time or offer them a reward for donations. These incentives are as varied as businesses. You might offer packages for different size contributions, anything from free meals to a catered event to stock to some percentage ownership of the business. Here, too, it will be helpful to look into what other people have offered and, odd as it might seem, to be creative with your offerings.

Crowdfunding campaigns operate most effectively through digital "word of mouth" sharing. If you are offering something unique that appeals, in particular, to individuals within a targeted age range, they will be more likely to share this information with their online contacts and increase your number of contributors. If you go with this option, you can select from several existing platforms. Each has different requirements, costs, and restrictions, so do your research to determine which best matches your needs.

It is possible to secure financing entirely through a single avenue; however, we find that small businesses that utilize multiple financing sources tend to achieve their monetary goals quickest. It is up to you which route, or how many, you pursue. Just remember to follow through. When people are investing, they expect a higher level of communication that you might be comfortable with at first. It might help to put yourself in their shoes. If you were, in effect, paying for a future product, you would be unsettled by radio silence. Plan to give regular updates to inform your investors of your progress, even if nothing has changed dramatically. Give them evidence of the work you are putting in to reward their faith in you. By remaining accountable, you also keep those avenues open for future investments.

A bonus of a successful crowdfunding campaign is that it will help generate buzz surrounding your business. For this reason, it is smart to have at least the basics of your branding worked out before crowdfunding. Another upside, these campaigns are interest-free and can be run concurrently with whatever other financing options you are pursuing.

The Nitty Gritty Numbers

But how much will you need to raise? As you start out, financial needs can seem quite nebulous. After calculating the costs of the truck, sales software and hardware, food preparation and storage devices, utilities, wages and training, supplies, permits, working capital, and maintenance costs, not to mention the cost of the food itself, your head is likely swimming. Your financial needs depend upon your business plan and approach and will vary significantly, but it is safe to assume that you will require a bare minimum of $30,000 to get running, more likely somewhere between $50,000 and $100,000. This may seem like a lot but consider the payoff.

Food trucks are a growth industry and more affordable than running a restaurant, which is why they are sometimes used as a starting point for someone looking to earn enough to eventually open a physical location. Moreover, food trucks generate an average of $300,000. Of course, getting a food truck to this point requires a significant amount of time and effort, but those investments can certainly pay off. We dive deeper into the numbers in later chapters. For now, consider how close to average the cost of living is for your area to give you a sense of how these statistics might reflect your costs. In places like New York City, permit and licensing costs will be significantly higher, though you might have more competitive options among your suppliers.

We recommend that you compile a comprehensive list of the startup costs for your region. Use the internet to research the specific costs of each aspect of your food truck business and their associated costs. This will give you an overall number to match or exceed as you begin to pursue financing.

Chapter 2: Your Creative Concept

Your Brand

If you have ever walked down a sidewalk and paused for a longer look at a sign or work of elaborate street art or even an unusually painted or decal-ornamented car, you understand the visual impact of aesthetics. This awareness comes more naturally to some people, but it is not necessary to effectively branding your business. People tend to mistakenly equate branding with design. While brand design, which includes elements like logo and font, is an important aspect of your food truck brand, it is not everything.

In fact, your brand is not something physical, though it includes physical elements. Your brand is an intangible concept that encompasses and defines your business. It should be everything you want your food truck to mean to people, though this might be primarily founded in aesthetics or on some sort of theme, such as a period in time (ex: Meg's Medieval Meats) or a more general concept (ex: Magical Macaroni). Unsurprisingly, effective branding is a powerful marketing tool and will help ensure your customers' commitment to and continued patronage of your food truck.

If you feel you already have a fully realized concept for your truck ready to go, feel free to skip ahead a bit. However, if you are like most, you will require at least a little brainstorming. We also do not want to assume that you have given your food truck creative concept any thought; you may simply be intrigued by the business model. However far you have come creatively, it is worth completing and testing your creative ideas. If you are starting from zero and need some inspiration, social media sites like Pinterest are a great place to start. On Pinterest, for example, various users have already collected ideas on their digital boards in the same way you might pin notes to a physical corkboard. Many of these boards are even specific to food trucks!

Of course, everyone's mind works a little differently. You may think best by collecting random inspirational thoughts in a notebook throughout the day or even using a dream journal. Perhaps you think best collaboratively and need to take a friend or two out for coffee to talk about possible ideas. At this point, you have a whole range of creative approaches to consider. Ideally, your brand will unite your personality and menu into a cohesive whole. When brainstorming, branch out to consider the things that make you and your neighborhood unique in addition to your favorite foods or unique family recipes.

If you are stuck, consider doing a little canvassing to ask what sorts of food people in your area might want to purchase from a food truck and why. Take your time working out your creative concept since this will inform a lot of the decisions you make going forward, everything from menu choices to truck design and naming.

Before long, you will begin to solidify your idea for your truck, or at least the basics. You should also understand your market and what type of custom food will appeal most to it. Now, you have the beginnings of a business plan worked out and, if you do not already have funding, you have a sense of how you might accomplish this. We will dig into branding strategies soon, but for now, consider your food truck concept as a unified whole.

Think about what makes your food truck offering unique and how you can structure every customer-facing aspect of your truck around it. There are many ways to do this. You might consider incorporating a unique local place name to tie your truck to the community, for example. Your concept need not originate with your food, but it should work with or complement the food you plan to serve. That said, there are plenty of successful trucks that rely more heavily on their cuisine or aesthetic appeal than on a unified brand. You can be successful without cohesive branding; however, it is easier to make consistent business decisions and to market your truck to customers when you have a well-defined brand.

Consider a few of your favorite restaurants. The chances are that you can describe them with only one or two words, not needing any more than this to distinguish them from other places you eat. Something about them stands out. It might be a signature dish or dessert that keeps you coming back again and again. It might be the unique diner aesthetic that calls up a sense of nostalgia. It might simply be the friendly and accommodating owner who remembers your name and favorite drink every time you come in. It might be that this restaurant is the only place within a hundred miles that serves traditional Ethiopian cuisine. You want your future customers to be able to do this with your food truck, to immediately create a positive association that sticks in their memory. Refining this easily identifiable concept now will work in your favor as you begin more comprehensive branding.

Considering Every Angle

Remember that local regulations will impact your concept, and it is worth doing some preliminary research before you become too invested in an idea that, for whatever reason, will not pass these regulations. For example, some areas restrict open flames in food trucks. Others limit the space a food truck may occupy when set up. Some simple internet searching should provide you with the basics of what is and is not permitted in your area.

Additionally, your creative food offerings should be something manageable and practical for production at a reasonably rapid rate. As much as we sympathize with the desire to offer something totally new, remember that people draw on associations. If your cuisine is too far from something recognizable as food, it might be difficult to draw in new customers. Essentially, be certain that your food appeals, no matter what it is. Without curious customers, the whole business falls apart.

In all likelihood, you know your brand already, whether you realize it or not. You did some of this work already when considering how best to describe your business. You know what drives you, where your passions are. If you thrive on customer interactions, consider putting yourself at the center of your brand. If you love food, focus on offering great taste. If you are artsy, put your emphasis on creative design and aesthetics. Whatever your strengths, now you get to flesh out that concept into a fully realized brand that will define your food truck moving forward. Start by looking at your goal statement again and reminding yourself of why you are doing this. Everything will spring from here.

Practical Design

Your logo and truck will be the most visible aspect of your food truck business. Our branding chapter will dig into the various options available to you, but for now, consider the visual impact of your truck. A simple logo and color palette can communicate far more to your customer base than just the name of your truck. If your branding is done well, it accomplishes a significant portion of your marketing for you. As your best means of drawing in customers on the street, it should be just as appealing as your food. What does this mean? When investing in a physical truck and trying to look for the best value, keep in mind the importance of aesthetics for a food truck. People are more likely to try food from a truck with a clean appearance and appealing design than from one that is dented or rusty without a large or visible logo that communicates what the truck offers.

If you are on a particularly tight opening budget, it may be best to open your truck to generate some revenue and use it to pay a professional design team to help you plan a rebranding. However, if you can do this work ahead of time, you will save needing to rebrand later. Either way, when in doubt with branding, it is best to start simple; any additional details can be filled in later. It is far easier to continue building on top of a solid structure than to try to go back and reshape that supporting framework.

As with any significant construction project, it is wise to consult a professional when it comes to building your food truck. Food truck builders can help you design your truck to optimize its limited space for your exact needs. Some food truck builders include a branding package to help you create a truck design that offers a strong visual representation of your brand. These builders know their industry and understand how to target your customer market, but any decision you make should be driven by your brand and truck goals. The better grasp you have on your brand, the better you will be able to communicate what you want from your truck's visual design. Understanding your brand will even give you a hand in making hiring decisions later. For example, if upbeat and engaging customer interaction is a key component of your brand, this is something you will want to look for in potential hires.

As you can see, there is a lot more that goes into your food truck plan than just the number crunching and physical purchases. Consider, too, the digital face of your business. More than anything in today's environment, an online presence is a must. The most successful food truck actively engages with customers through social media platforms and understands how to leverage digital promotions. We will look at specific digital necessities for your truck in the coming chapters; for now, it is important just to be aware that this will be part of your business.

You may have limited digital literacy or be unfamiliar with social media and web content. If this is the case, set aside extra funds in your budget to bring in an expert who can translate your food truck brand into digital spaces and make the most of the marketing opportunities provided by the internet. Any quality marketing approach will include a website SEO (Search Engine Optimization) strategy that will ensure your brand is promoted through relevant internet searches.

Marketing is all about converting all these strategies into sales, but do not stress about the details yet. Most important is to get your food truck running to spread awareness of your brand. Then you can fine-tune your approach to account for observations you are able to make about your customer base. For instance, if your average customer age is younger than the averages for restaurants in your area, you can capitalize on this difference by investing in digital products and services that are most likely to reach your potential customer age bracket.

Knowing When to Outsource

As a small business owner, it is easy to get caught up in financial concerns and do as much as possible yourself to save time and money. However, your brand defines who you are to your customers, so it is worth investing in professional help with your design and logo especially. A good branding team will help you create a palette of colors, basic graphics, and fonts that pair with your logo to provide instant recognition. If you like, you need not go further than your computer. Many brand companies offer affordable packages that include setting up a basic website where you can begin to market your brand before you even open. It is also helpful to have a package like this put together if you decide to begin a crowdfunding campaign to give the many people who will be exposed to your brand online something concrete and appealing to support.

Though we are discussing digital expertise specifically, bear in mind that there will be many aspects of starting your own business where you will feel out of your depth. Do not be afraid of this feeling. If you can acknowledge where you need guidance, you will be better equipped to learn and bring in the expert help that will make your business a success.

As we mentioned, the digital presence of your truck is an impactful variable in your truck's branding equation. Many platforms can help you maintain relationships with your customers, including a website, blog, and accounts on such social media sites as Instagram, Twitter, Facebook, and FourSquare, a platform that provides location-based information to users. Other downloadable phone apps like Roaming Hunger allow customers to track the movements of their favorite food trucks. Do some investigating to discover which applications are most used by your target customers. Be aware that not all apps are active in all areas. Often, you can contact app owners to discuss how both parties will benefit; for example, you might offer to promote the application that allows your customers to track your truck with visual or digital advertising.

Beginning with a solid brand is important. So, if you are unable to afford professional branding based on what you have already raised or plan to raise to start your truck, consider a separate crowdfunding campaign to fund your branding. These investments now can result in higher sales later.

Truck Decor

Your truck is a key component of this overall design. It serves a dual purpose, actively advertising even as you serve your customers. Essentially, you can consider your truck as an around-the-clock advertising space. When you acquire your truck, you will have options for altering its appearance to match your brand, scaled to size. The most common of these are vinyl wrap and painting. Vinyl wrap allows for crisp detail and images since the wraps are printed before being applied to your truck. As an added benefit, they are sealed and tend to last for years. They are a common choice because they also offer a layer of weather protection for your truck, which will likely spend the majority of its time outside. Wraps can be expensive, running anywhere from $3000-$5000, so look for a provider that offers a warranty on your wrap.

If this seems a bit beyond your price range right now, consider simplifying the look of your truck. You might have your truck painted a single color and apply a simple, smaller wrap for just your logo or a single image. If you do opt to get your truck painted, hire a professional. It may sound simple enough to paint the flat surfaces of your truck, but the differences between a professional and amateur paint job stand out. Professional paint jobs are also far more likely to last and withstand the elements. If you are operating your truck in an especially hot and sunny climate, consider opting for vinyl or a base of a solid color of paint. Nothing fades and damages paint color faster than sun exposure.

Remember, your truck is the face of your brand. It will set you apart, and its colors and design are what your customers will picture when they think of your brand. When I say Nike, you visualize their classic swoosh. The same goes for any number of successful brands. So, this choice between paint and vinyl will depend more than anything on the design approach you decide upon. Certain looks will communicate your brand better than others. In the same vein, certain logos will transfer to the side of a food truck far more effectively using printed vinyl material. As we will consider further in future chapters, many factors will play into your visual branding decisions, including potential community engagement issues.

Marketing Strategy

Branding is more than custom design or appearance or even your truck, though these are important aspects of your food truck business. A comprehensive brand creates trust between you and your customers. This involves your social media presence and face-to-face customer interactions. The visual design elements that support your brand, in fact, only communicate aspects of your brand. Your brand only fully exists in its relationship with your customers. You grow this relationship with every interaction you have with those customers. Every time they see your truck or logo, view your menu on your website, speak with your staff while ordering food, or post reviews or pictures of their meals on social media.

As you will discover, there are even mobile applications you can purchase or subscribe to which will allow your customers to track your truck's location. In all your customer interactions, however, whether digital or real-world, it is important to maintain consistency. Some of the most successful food trucks built their marketing campaigns on their story. That is, they used their owner's inspirational story, motivations, and struggles to realize their dream as part of the foundation of their brand. Stories like this have a lasting impact, so consider incorporating your unique origin story into your online presence in particular.

The Campbell Soup Company, for example, was one of the first and most consistent to successfully engage through social media by adopting and maintaining a specific friendly, humorous tone. Part of crafting your brand with the help of a designer or team will involve selecting a level of formality. With any food truck, this range is slightly limited. It is difficult to maintain a true black-tie atmosphere while serving food to customers on the sidewalk. Of course, playing with formality may fit your brand. Black-tie Burgers, anyone?

No matter how you choose to express and define your brand identity, be certain to maintain consistency. It is this familiarity that your customers will return to as you establish relationships with them and increase their confidence in what you offer. Planting the seeds of this brand loyalty early on can only help you in the long run. Say, for instance, a customer's order was wrong. If this is only the first time such a mistake has occurred in their experience with your truck, they are far less likely to spread a negative review than if it is their only experience and association with your truck. Crowdfunding campaigning will not buy you customer loyalty; however, it can lay a strong foundation for it before your wheels ever hit the road.

Chapter 3: Sales

Profit Margins

One of the first things you discover in running a food truck is that your business, at every level, will be sales-driven. Your orders are what keeps your food truck in operation. This sounds like common sense but actually is much more. Consider where those sales come from. There are many factors that determine how accessible and appealing your truck is to customers. Plus, there are many factors beyond your control involved in operating a food truck.

For instance, the weather will have a huge impact on your sales, so you will need to capitalize on every sunny day. You will learn to track your customer volume to make the most of the time you are open. You will also begin to understand the draw of special events and festivals, despite the overhead expenses, because food truck profit margins are usually under 10%, so you need to find ways to ensure a steady flow of customers. Your ideal day will be busy from start to finish.

For your business purposes, sales refer to the total amount of money you make selling your food. Your profit margin is the percentage of that amount that remains after you have accounted for all of your expenses, including labor, parking and permits, food and food waste, fuel and maintenance, marketing, and anything else you have to pay for to keep your truck in operation. It is relatively simple for you to calculate your margins, and it is a good idea to remain aware of them. Not only can a low margin prompt you to consider cost-saving options, calculating your margin gives you advance information on whether or not you will be able to make loan or lease payments and whether you will be able to begin saving for additional marketing or other costs.

Be sure to pick a set period of time to track your sales and expenses to accurately calculate your profit margins. Many small business owners use tracking software that generates reports on a monthly basis to cut out the time it might otherwise take to generate these figures.

Digital Tools

Point of Sale

A necessary item you will need to purchase is some form of POS (Point Of Sale) system to record customer orders and accept payment, such as a credit card reader, printer, and the associated software for processing payments. Many small businesses find that a tablet with a card and touchless payment reader attachment, called a terminal, meets their needs. Various annual and monthly subscription services cater to the POS needs of small businesses, and it is important to do your research. Some even offer complete POS systems for a single upfront payment. One of your best resources in such cases is other food truck owners. We will discuss some ways of connecting with these individuals within your business community in a later chapter.

For now, bear in mind that operating a food truck presents unique demands depending on your location. Befriending someone already in the know may give you a jump start, allowing you to learn from some of their methods and approaches. Whatever the case, as with any new business, there will be a certain amount of trial and error. Embrace this. Nothing is perfect the first time. As you grow your business, you will discover new and better ways of running your truck. This is part of the experience and only made less frustrating by your attitude towards the learning process.

Certain newer systems are even designed specifically for food trucks and similar operations, such as Square. Some such services charge higher processing fees than others, particularly software aimed at larger operations, but one of the benefits of these systems is that it is relatively easy to switch to a different POS system if you find that your current system is not a good fit or is not keeping up with your business demands. Touchless or single-touch systems may simplify transactions for your staff as well, increasing their productivity and efficiency by enabling them to spend less time on this part of each sale. This is particularly important in a food truck setting, where space is limited and the number of employees who can work inside the truck at any one time is limited by regulations and safety concerns.

Customer Relationship Management

Profit margins are only one of many ways to translate your sales data into information that makes sense to you and which you can act on. As you get comfortable running your food truck, it may also be worth investing in free or paid Customer Relationship Management (CRM) platforms designed for small businesses. Various software programs are available to help you streamline your sales by analyzing patterns in your sales history and inventory. Some software combines these offerings with marketing software. You will need to search to find the software that best matches your food truck sales demands.

Though you might not need or be able to afford it at first, CRM software is a great option for consolidating your sales and customer information and managing it as those numbers get higher. It is a great way to inform your marketing choices, such as which demographics to target with certain campaigns, and often includes some marketing software for managing and increasing your website traffic and customer lists.

CRMs offer a range of tools. Most CRM software like Microsoft Dynamics are oriented toward larger businesses, and some include accounting software as one of many features. Platforms like Salesforce allow you to track and manage employee wages and scheduling as well as sales. More direct spreadsheet software like QuickBooks operates as a kind of digital accountant on your behalf. With these programs, you input your data (by linking accounts, this may even happen automatically), and the software processes it into reports as simple or detailed as you prefer. CRMs aim to find solutions that will ultimately increase your sales by giving you as much information about those sales as possible. When and where they come from, for example, and even what percentage of those sales are return customers. Many CRMs include tools to help you with digital marketing as well.

Your choice of software will depend on a number of factors, including how long a system takes to set up. Cloud-based software involves less lead time. Look at the support offered by each software to give your future self an extra hand in resolving any technical issues. You should also consider how user-friendly the software is. Those sales data reports are useless to you if you cannot easily understand them and translate them into increased sales. Look at sample graphs and other data visualization offered by each software to compare ease of use. Of course, the cost of the software will be an important factor in your decision since most CRMs are subscription-based and will require you to add an additional cost to your monthly budget. Free trials are a good way to get a feel for if a product is cost-effective. Some of the most highly rated CRMs currently on offer for small businesses include Drip, Constant Contact, Salesflare, Pipedrive, Salesforce, Freshsales, HubSpot, Streak, and Agile.

Cash

Food trucks tend to handle more cash than many small businesses, so be prepared for all forms of payment, including stocking your cash drawer with the necessary change each day. As simple as it might seem to choose a cash-only or no cash option, these approaches directly translate into lost sales. Moreover, if you ever do have an issue with one form of payment or the other, it is wise to have a backup option you can rely upon temporarily while your cash drawer gets repaired or your software is debugged.

This, in fact, brings up another relevant point. POS systems include built-in security, but it is important to install and keep antivirus software on your business computers and any other devices you use up to date. Think of these costs as protecting your investment in the hardware and software that keep your business running smoothly and safeguarding your trust relationship with your customers.

For a food truck, the ideal sales software will be affordable, small business-oriented, insured, and include POS and CRM functionality. For now, only the POS is necessary, but bear in mind that CRM features will be useful as you build your sales and increase your customer base.

Whatever software you choose, be sure to track your sales and expenses. It is valuable to you as a touchpoint for how well you are meeting your business goals and where you might need to make changes. Besides, come tax season, you will need this information!

Projections

The sales projections you include in your executive summary will be based on data from businesses in similar situations to yours. Forecasting your sales is neither science nor pure guesswork; though there is no exact formula, you can make an informed estimate based on facts gathered from similar businesses, like the average customer counts for other mobile vendors in the area. Another relevant factor here is the length of time it takes to prepare each meal. The shorter the turnaround, the more customers can be served each day. This number also allows you to project the maximum number of customers you could serve each hour during peak hours.

If you can prepare each menu item in 5 minutes, you will be able to serve 12 customers each hour. If you are open for two shifts of four hours each, you will be able to serve 96 customers in a day. If you charge $6 for each meal, your maximum daily revenue is $576. For an accurate forecast, you would take a percentage of this number to account for weather conditions and breakdowns, as well as any of the many other issues that might interrupt customer flow. Taking 80% of your maximum revenue would put your estimated daily revenue at approximately $460. If you are open six days a week, you can conservatively estimate your monthly revenue at around $11,000. Obviously, this calculation will get slightly more complicated if your menu prices vary or if other mobile vendors communicate that certain days of the week yield extremely slow sales or if certain times of day generate more foot traffic.

In general, as a food truck business owner, you will need to pay close attention to your customer flow to determine how to maximize customer's access to your truck. For some trucks, this may mean relocating partway through the day. For example, you might park near a busy bus stop in the morning and then move across from a park or college during lunch hours before moving again to be near a subway station where lots of commuters will pass your truck on their way home from work. Your daily, weekly, and even seasonal routes will depend on your area, so plan to put in time planning routes and reworking them based on your sales, or lack thereof.

On the expenses side, you can do the same. Based on your estimated customer count, you can calculate the cost of each meal to estimate your food expenses for the day. Adding your labor costs per hour and fuel and parking costs per day will give you a good sense of your minimum daily expenses. These calculations will inform your inventory as well, so separately breaking down various food and beverage items will help ensure you stay appropriately stocked to meet demand.

Various templates, called financial projection templates, are available for purchase online. These will allow you to simply plug in your estimated figures to generate simple visual charts of your estimated sales. Some are even designed specifically for food trucks! Of course, if you have the time, it can give you a more solid grasp of your own business's bottom line to perform these calculations yourself. That said, calculating annual sales forecasts from this information can be tricky, and it is wise to consult with experts (in this case, other food truck owners familiar with sales patterns across the year) when making an annual projection. Consider that certain snowy months might put your truck out of commission for weeks at a time, depending on your location.

Once your truck is operational, these sales projections will provide a good watermark for your initial success. If, after several months, you are failing to meet your projections, it is probably a smart idea to take a step back to figure out why. If you need to generate new projections, do so. However, it may be possible to streamline your operations to cut down on some per-meal costs.

As part of your three-year forecast, you will need to demonstrate your food truck business has the capacity to grow by at least 10%, ideally closer to 25%, each year. Forecasting your sales by multiplying by the lower end of this spectrum will help ensure you can meet your sales goals while keeping your investors' faith in your ability to deliver.

It is important to remember that, though you are dependent upon sales, becoming hyper-focused on profit can draw your attention away from what defines your brand. When you can balance your drive for profit with your passion for your truck, you will be able to maximize your productivity. Why? Not because you are making money, although no one will argue with that distinct benefit. Rather, you will be fulfilling your goals as an owner of a food truck business and passing that sense of fulfillment along. When your customers connect with you, they will keep coming back. As you will see, your efficiency and marketing strategies will have a direct impact on this customer relationship.

Booking

Though any offerings outside of basic food service will not be feasible at first, it is important to start thinking about the future growth of your food truck early. Projections are a great place to start, as they allow you to consider how much additional revenue you might be able to fold back into your business as you invest in new marketing, products, or services that will help you continue to expand.

One of the simplest ways to ensure your food truck remains profitable in your off-season or on slower days is to allow individuals and companies to book your truck for private events or catering during times when you know you can expect reduced foot traffic. Booking for groups in predetermined, larger numbers allows you to maximize your profits during those periods, as well, since you can guarantee the use of set quantities of ingredients and charge a small fee for exclusivity.

Whether or not you offer these services at first, it is important that you keep a calendar of availability for your truck. If you apply for a festival or other event, be sure to block out those days to prevent conflicts and consider in advance how you will arrange staffing and wages for those events.

At first, it may be simplest to set up bookings via phone. However, seamless online booking options will expand your reach in the long run. Many websites include templates for setting up your own booking preferences and availability, which is a worthwhile investment for most food trucks. More applications can be added to an existing website. Remember to make certain your website and any other digital applications are optimized for mobile use.

In general, in today's world, a quality website is a solid investment, but even this depends on your vision for your business and the model that best matches your customer base. It is possible that the majority of your customers are walk-ups on the street and that you have an extremely low average wait time. In this case, you might choose to put more money toward the visual impact of your physical truck rather than maintaining a quality online presence. Over time, you may even adjust your approach to match what your sales data is telling you about your customers. For instance, you may discover a surprisingly high percentage of cash sales on weekdays and adjust your register and staff schedule accordingly.

A significant portion of your customers will use their mobile devices to access your website, particularly first-time visitors who are simply searching for available food options nearby. Making certain it is easy to navigate your website is key for landing those sales. Along with this, keeping your website updated and ensuring that search engines are generating the correct hours, locations, and contact information for your food truck will promote customer trust in your brand and reliably bring in business.

Leveraging Reviews

Online platforms also allow you to leverage positive customer reviews. Not only can you feature exceptionally positive customer feedback and comments on your website and social media feeds, but rating systems are an important factor in people's decision to eat at your truck or not. You can curate your website ratings, but be aware that dissatisfied customers have many ways to make their opinions known online. Various sites allow customers to rank their experiences, so it is important to follow your online reviews with alerts and consider making changes if you are noticing consistently negative reviews. A food truck experience is more than simply paying and eating. Interactions with your staff will directly impact how a customer remembers their meal experience.

If you are struggling to bring in the number of customers you need each week to meet your financial obligations, consider introducing some form of loyalty reward. Such as a punch card to promote repeat business. You may also offer an incentive to review your truck online, such as a free drink with your meal. Especially at first, do not try to introduce too many special deals. Keep it simple and work on building your customer base. One of the best ways is to keep detailed records of your business each day, recording location and weather conditions to allow you to analyze sales patterns and optimize your business each day by planning where and when your truck should park.

Chapter 4: Finances

Whether or not you have prior experience running a small business, establishing good record keeping and working toward profitability while balancing the daily demands of operating a food truck can seem overwhelming. Plenty of accounting software options can provide you with the means of simplifying your finances. For example, Intuit offers QuickBooks, specifically designed for small business owners. Simple online video courses can also help you refresh your bookkeeping skills. As we covered in the previous chapter, quality POS and CRM software for small businesses will accurately record and account for your sales and provide valuable resources for managing employees and customers.

But all of this comes later after you have acquired the financing to purchase your truck and equipment, not to mention covering the many fees required for setting up a legal food truck business. Your initial financing will need to cover your startup and monthly costs for at least two months until you are able to consistently bring in revenue.

It can be tempting to fold all your revenue back into your business at first, but we encourage you to resist the temptation. Keep yourself on the payroll and build up an emergency fund for your business before reinvesting in more products, services, or marketing opportunities. It is also critical not to shy away from loans designed to help get your business off the ground. When you plan your billing strategy well, you will have no problem maintaining good business credit and making your payments on time. The size of your initial loans will, of course, impact how long it takes to pay them off. Carefully consider your repayment plan, too, since you will need to cover these costs out of your food truck profits. As we will discuss later, when considering your menu pricing, it is important to ensure you are covering your expenses beyond ingredients and staff wages. While it is wise to offer competitive pricing, you must consider a cash flow strategy that will drive your business success.

First things first: Let's investigate the various options you should consider for your startup financing. Take your time looking into opportunities specific to your area, too. There may be significant tax incentives that make certain small business loans a better approach than a crowdfunding campaign, for example. Before you begin any applications, be sure your executive summary from the first chapter is polished and ready to go. Many investors will want to meet with and interview you. Putting in the time to memorize your business plan is a great idea to help boost your confidence and convince investors that you have thoughtfully considered how to make your food truck profitable.

Loans and Financing

Online loan aggregators can match loan options to your requirements, and you will likely require a balance of several financing options. Different parts of your food truck business are eligible for different forms of financing, and you may find that some or all of these are applicable to your situation. Many online loan aggregators will give you access to loans that might not be offered by traditional banks. They look at more than your business credit score (which you will not have yet), often do not require collateral, and offer lower minimum amounts.

Sites like Credibly and LendingTree can give you a sense of the many small business loan options, but there are several lenders recommended specifically for food truck businesses. We advise using a search engine like LendingTree's ValuePenguin to search for specific small business loans based on the amount you need, your credit score, and the type and age of your business. Using a search engine like this cuts out a lot of wasted effort spent following up on loans that do not match your needs since they classify loans based on whether they are best for startups, expansions, businesses with poor credit, or simply acquiring working capital. In fact, payment-processing companies like PayPal and Square are also great options if you require a smaller, one-year loan as working capital for your first months of operation. If you already use one of these payment processors, definitely consider going this route.

As a general overview, an aggregator might suggest that if you are looking to lease your truck and equipment, you should consider Crest Capital. For purchasing a new truck, National Funding might be a better option. If you need a flexible loan that you can pay back in a shorter period of time, LoanBuilder and LightStream offer loans that can match your needs. But your situation might be different. Perhaps your existing business has less than ideal credit, in which case you should look into lenders like Fora Financial or OnDeck for a short-term loan that can give you the cash injection necessary to revitalize your food truck business.

Remember, the best loan for you will depend on your situation. Though we have provided many options to consider, you may find that another lender makes more sense for your situation. A local bank, for instance, might be more willing to consider a small loan to help support a local business. Also, loan applications take time and require work to prepare, so be certain before you apply and organize your materials in advance to avoid making costly mistakes.

Equipment financing

Larger commercial equipment, including appliances and vehicles, used by businesses are eligible for financing at low rates of interest since the equipment itself serves as collateral. The large appliance elements of your truck and the truck itself can be financed this way. As with personal vehicles, consider depreciation when deciding between new and refurbished equipment.

So, where do you find equipment loans? The answer might surprise you since, generally, it is the company selling or reselling the equipment that offers the financing directly. There are some banks that offer equipment financing, though going through a bank may lengthen the application process. Certain companies also operate exclusively as equipment financers or operate as online lenders. These include Balboa Capital, Currency Finance, Crest Capital, CIT, and eLease.com.

For food truck businesses, equipment financing is often the best approach for covering as much of your overhead cost as possible because the financing process is fast and offers low-interest rates. These rates stay low because the equipment itself serves as collateral. Of course, this means defaulting on payments could result in repossession of your truck, which is an important aspect of equipment financing to consider. Equipment financing lenders also tend to place less emphasis on credit. This option is available to businesses that do not have the credit scores necessary to qualify for certain other loans. Most lenders that offer equipment financing offer equipment leasing as well, usually with the option to purchase once the lease term is up. Again, this process operates almost exactly as it does with personal vehicles. Leasing, however, tends to require higher rates of interest, closer to 12% rather than the average equipment financing of 5%.

One important consideration involved in equipment financing is that, as in the restaurant business, technology advances can rapidly render your equipment obsolete. You do not want to be stuck with outdated equipment, particularly if your cuisine is something newer or you must capitalize on current trends. Another consideration is that some larger equipment financing requires a 10% down payment, so you will likely also need to find another lender or investor first.

For most equipment financing applications, you will need to provide a valid driver's license, voided check for your business account, bank statements going back at least three months, your credit score, most recent business tax return, and a quote for the equipment you want to finance. These requirements will vary based on who is offering the equipment financing. Be sure to verify that you have everything you need before beginning any application!

Business microloans

Small business loan opportunities vary dramatically by country, but your federal government website is always a great place to start looking for your options. In the United States, SBA 7a microloans or other small business-specific microloans are generally defined as any loan under $50,000, an amount too small for most banks to offer. These are ideal for small businesses because of their flexibility. Though the application process takes longer than that of many other loans, the funds can be used for supplies, equipment, working capital, or inventory; essentially, any aspect of your food truck business. This might allow you to cover multiple financial needs from a single loan, helping keep your payments consolidated.

An SBA loan is technically a subcategory within the larger grouping of microloans, which are specifically intended to provide access to underserved populations. A great example is Opportunity Fund, which serves primarily women-owned and minority-owned small businesses since these business owners often have limited access to traditional loan opportunities. Different microloan companies target different small business owners, so you will likely be able to easily find a microlender that closely matches your exact needs. Be sure you understand the requirements for microloans, however, since you may need to provide collateral and to personally guarantee the loan amount.

Lines of business credit

As part of establishing your business and similar in repayment to a credit card, you may need the working capital that comes from opening these lines of credit with banks or other lenders in predetermined amounts. A line of credit lets your business access capital as you need it, rather than in advance as with loans. When starting a food truck business, you will likely not know the exact amount of working capital you will need. Getting approved for a large amount will allow you to use your credit as needed, say if you are unable to get equipment financing for a grill that you need to begin operations.

Like a credit card, you will have monthly payments, but your credit limit may be much higher depending on the terms and your credit rating, anywhere between $10,000 and $1,000,000. Even if you do not need it right away, if possible, you should open a line of business credit as a form of extra security; if you do not end up needing it, great! But it is smart to have the option in case you do end up needing it. Also, if you are looking to build good business credit, timely repayment is a great way to accomplish this.

Business credit cards

Though subject to higher interest rates and shorter repayment periods, these cards are a useful tool for any small business. Any business will face last-minute or emergency charges that a credit card can help cover in the short term. When choosing a business credit card, look at introductory or rewards offers that you might benefit from. If you plan lots of travel with your truck, for example, a card with bonuses for travel-related charges might be a smart choice. These cards are another way you can build up good credit. You will need to be aware of the exact terms of your card. We recommend setting up electronic payments to ensure you do not miss any and damage your credit rating. The card with the best rewards for your food truck business will depend on the types of purchases you plan to use it for.

Most major credit card companies offer credit cards specifically for business use. Capital One, American Express, and Chase offer particularly good rates for small businesses. However you choose to set up your business banking and cards, it is important to separate your business accounts from your personal accounts and be aware of who has access to your business accounts and cards.

Crowdfunding campaigns

We discussed crowdfunding in-depth in the first chapter, but it is important to remember that this option is available to you to fund any aspect of your food truck business. It offers an alternative to more traditional forms of financing and is increasingly the first choice for small businesses. The primary benefit is that your campaign creates hype and generates awareness of your business and brand while giving you access to funds interest-free. A crowdfunding campaign is a much larger time and effort commitment than other loan applications. Be sure you plan how you want to approach such a campaign and have prepared a timeline.

We mentioned before that these campaigns tend to be most successful when you are able to commit funds to develop your brand before beginning a campaign. This way, your campaign serves a dual purpose as free advertising. You are often also able to begin compiling customer email lists and social media connections during crowdfunding. Having a cohesive social media and digital marketing strategy in place will help you maximize the benefit of your campaign. It is worth noting, too, that you do not need to crowdfund exclusively for startup costs. You might be interested in rebranding your food truck or acquiring capital to expand in some way later. So long as you have a clearly defined and realistic goal that you can articulate well, you should be able to find supporters to back your campaign.

Depending on how you have financed your truck, you will likely have some form of interest payment you will need to make each month in addition to your payroll and other obligations. This is important for maintaining your credit rating and needs to be a priority. A history of paying on time also impacts your ability to acquire future lines of credit to support your business. Based on your credit, you may be able to use an installment loan to cover employee wages at first, though interest rates tend to be higher.

As you see, there are many financing options for your food truck. However, there are more considerations involved in taking on loan responsibilities than just weighing the benefits of each financing option, as we covered in the previous chapters. For instance, there may be simple ways to boost your credit score before applying for loans that would increase your likelihood of success. If you have a concern about your credit rating, consider using a free or paid online credit score reporting service to help you figure out how to reach the necessary score. Even if you do not initially take out a loan requiring a credit report, it is wise to work toward a credit score of at least 600 just in case you do need to take out a loan after getting your food truck operating. Ideally, you should shoot for a 720 score, though for many reasons, this can be difficult to maintain.

One of the ideal ways to keep your credit healthy is to ensure any payments you are responsible for are paid on time. If you cannot make a payment, be proactive and contact your lender to see if it is possible to refinance and work out a different repayment plan that will fit better with your monthly earnings. This way, though you may pay more in the long run, you avoid damaging your credit and remove the stress of failing to meet the demands of your budget. Maintaining awareness of your finances and responsibly handling money are the best things you can do to give your food truck business its best possible start and keep it operating smoothly. Remember that you will also have a responsibility to your employees and the owners of the businesses from whom you source your ingredients and supplies.

If you are not confident in your money management skills or simply have little experience with handling business finances, there are many free online courses that can give you a basic understanding of the key elements of financial responsibility. As we have said before, it is also wise to hire an expert to handle your books and accounting software, particularly once your business takes off and the demands on your time increase.

Debt Burden

Whether your business debt is in equipment financing, SBA microloans, lines of credit, credit cards, crowdfunding, or some combination of all these options, any small business can expect to require startup loans. What is important is maintaining a manageable balance while moving toward profitability. In the meantime, working capital can be hard to come by as a new business. As we mentioned before, the best option in the U.S. may be an SBA loan, which offers a long repayment period. In the event that you need to default on a loan, the SBA does offer debt consolidation loans to protect small businesses.

But with a new small business, there is always the possibility that you need to take on a personal loan. This is an option to consider carefully based on the real dollar amounts being generated by your truck. If you can expect to pay off such a loan in a reasonable amount of time, it may be worth considering. Bear in mind that your present and future personal credit score will factor into this decision.

Budgeting and Financial Security

Even while balancing your finances, it is important to accumulate a safety net before upgrading equipment or introducing extra expenses that are not necessary to running your truck and effectively supporting your brand. As with any small business, you will not achieve profitability immediately. Opening separate business accounts from the outset will help simplify your budgeting.

While you will probably not be able to afford to pay an independent financial advisor at first, maintaining an updated budget will help alleviate the potential stress and worry surrounding your budget. Reports from your POS system will help with this effort. As your business expands or, conversely, if you are struggling to meet your financial commitments, it may be time to consider consulting with a professional.

Know your strengths and value your time. Even if you are a former CPA, it might not be cost-effective for you to spend your time putting together quarterly tax submissions. You may prefer creating your own formulas in an application like Excel, but there are also many templates available online designed to meet small business requirements. Then again, in your first business year, you might not have another option. Consider all the demands on your time and energy as a small business owner and schedule yourself a reasonable amount of time off. We get it. You are dedicated to making your food truck succeed. But you cannot accomplish this if you run yourself into the ground. Scheduling all the demands on your time will help you appreciate just how much you are getting done while helping you keep up with the many demands on your time.

Chapter 5: Personnel

Though it is one of the most vital components of your food truck business, staffing is one of the areas in which you have the most control and flexibility. Decide how you want the food production to function for your truck. This can help you determine how many staff positions you will need and the skills required for each one. Once you have your set staff and have worked out a schedule that works for your truck, bear in mind that you may still need to bring in additional temporary staff for catering events or festivals.

Your staff size will depend on the type of truck you are running, whether parts of your food need to be prepared beforehand in a commercial kitchen, and how often you plan to have your truck operating. As in restaurants and the rest of the food service industry, standard practice is to have "front of house" and "back of house" staff. These simply refer to whether or not the staff member is interacting with your customers and representing your brand with personal interactions or working behind the scenes and supporting your brand through the food products they help produce, cleaning tasks they perform, or with other maintenance and accounting work.

You will need to decide the role in which you will be able to maximize your contributions to your business. This may be as a back-of-house staffer who is responsible for multiple tasks. Whatever you decide works best for your truck, you will need to hire, which means you will need to have a solid sense of the number of people you need to have working for you (and whom you can afford to pay to do so). This last point is important for scheduling concerns. If your truck is operational more than eight hours a day on most days of the week, you will have multiple staff shifts to cover each day.

Some trucks that sell prepackaged foods operate with as few as one person, while other trucks require more than ten. The average, however, is for food truck business owners to have between two and eight employees, assuming you will work in your truck. If this is not the case for whatever reason, you will need an additional staff member that you trust to make bigger operational decisions working in your place.

As your business expands, you will bring in more back-of-house staff to maintain your books and marketing strategy. Your truck will be most successful with a full-time marketing individual on your payroll. You may need to work up to being able to afford this, and if you kicked off your food truck with an online campaign or branding package, you could likely hold off on filling this position immediately. However, growing your business in today's environment will hinge upon effective digital marketing. At some point, you will need to bring in a back-of-house staff member as a marketing associate. They will build your online followers through consistent social media engagement, website maintenance, and promotions through email or text subscription lists.

Hiring

Know what you are looking for in your staff before you begin the hiring process. What qualities matter most to you? The basic practical skills of food truck service can be learned. Looking for people who work as a team, communicate well, and can offer excellent customer service is a great place to start. If possible, find people who are excited by your food truck or are passionate about some aspect of your business. Perhaps they share a passion for the food truck industry.

You will be working closely with your first employees, so it is also important that they feel comfortable with you and respect your judgment. If you have never been someone's boss or been a manager before, consider putting in a little time reading or taking a free online course on how to manage well. Be patient with yourself, too. You will make mistakes. Everyone does! You need not be perfect or know how to do everything. One of the biggest mistakes people make in management positions is believing that they must have all the answers all the time. The more honest you are about when you need help or advice from an expert, the more open to learning you are, the better boss you will be.

There are many ways to gather a pool of applicants. The simplest of these involves posting your job openings, with a brief description of the job requirements and pay rate, on online job sites. There are even job boards exclusively catering to the food service industry, though often you must pay a small fee to post on more specialized sites. Consider posting your job openings as early as possible to allow for plenty of time for reviewing applications and setting up interviews with potential employees. Basic qualities you will likely look for, though you can certainly choose what characteristics matter most to you, are consistent professionalism and reliability. Prepare thoughtful interview questions in advance. It is wise to remind yourself of what you legally can and cannot ask, as well. Various interview templates exist online and make a good starting point.

You should begin thinking about setting a target opening date and informing anyone you intend to hire of the various tasks that might be required of them as part of getting your truck up and running. Do not overpromise. If you may not need your staff for full, consistent shifts until your food truck is operational, communicate with them to work out a schedule that meets both your needs. Your staff may start part-time and move to full-time work hours when your truck is ready to open.

Ready for an industry secret? Current food service employees are an untapped hiring market. There is a lot working in a food truck has to offer someone with experience working for a larger food service corporation. Even starting out, you may be able to pay more than the minimum wage offered to entry-level employees at chain restaurants. You may let your employees keep tips, for instance. The chances are that your uniform requirements will also be more relaxed. Generally, the environment itself will appeal to someone looking for more than the daily grind offered by a chain.

What does this mean for you? Any time you are ordering a coffee or fast-food meal, pay attention to the staff. If someone is particularly attentive or friendly? Start a conversation and tell them you are hiring. If you are uncomfortable doing this, practice with friends or family members. But, in our experience, this gives you an opportunity to get a true sense of how well you could work with another person and get an idea of their professional attitude and approach before they are trying to impress a potential employer.

Chef

Your business is, ultimately, a food business. Unless you yourself are a trained chef and plan to serve in this role in your truck, your first hiring step should be to invest in a qualified and skilled chef who can create the delicious food that will keep your customers coming back and spreading the word to their friends. However, this choice depends on the type of food you will be providing. A gourmet sandwich truck may not require paying a professional chef, which will be reflected in the cost passed on to the consumer. You will need to decide whether the type of cuisine you are providing requires bringing in a professional, someone with experience, or simply after-hire training.

We have mentioned the role of cook several times as something that your whole staff may need to assist with. However, it is important to consider how involved your meals will be and what training or certifications are required for anyone working directly with the food you serve.

Anyone preparing your food before it reaches your truck or inside your truck must have the appropriate health and safety certifications, which we will discuss in the next chapter. They must also receive adequate training in how you want your food served as a part of your brand. Does it matter if the sandwich wrap is folded in a certain way every time to prevent leakage?

It is likely that you will choose to hire an experienced chef to supervise some or most of the food preparation. A professional chef's culinary certifications generally give them the knowledge and skills to help train your other staff members and purchase supplies. It is wise to hire your chef or head cook first so that they can help you in arranging your truck to match your culinary demands. Ideally, you will find someone with experience in your type of food preparation or with other food truck experience to fill this role. They may recommend hiring back-of-house kitchen staff to prepare ingredients out of a commercial kitchen and clean and restock your truck each day. You will need to discuss what approach will work best for your food truck. For some trucks, kitchen staff work as both back-of-house and front of house employees.

This is entirely determined by your food truck arrangement. If, for example, you expand to operate multiple trucks, it may make more sense to have your food prepared in bulk in advance in a commercial-grade kitchen. These spaces can often be rented from restaurants or hotels during off-hours, or you may decide it is worth leasing or purchasing your own kitchen space.

Food service moves quickly. This is another reason that having a professional chef on your team matters. This chef will be able to handle the pace of food truck kitchens, which need to be able to fulfill orders with consistent speed. Your chef is also an excellent resource. If they are familiar with the food service industry in your area, they will be better equipped to recommend specific training for your staff or advise you on necessary certifications.

Driver

You are probably planning to drive your food truck yourself or have your manager share this role. However, you will need to consider the regulations for your area. In most areas, you must possess a commercial driver's license to operate a truck over a certain size. You will need to either obtain such a license yourself or ensure that at least one staff member is legally allowed to drive your truck each day. Some food trucks employ a separate driver. This depends in part on the arrangement and size of your truck, but generally, the course or training requirements for obtaining a commercial driver's license are not overly complex. As the owner or leaser of your food truck, we recommend getting your commercial license. Even if you will not be the primary operator, it is wise to have backup options just in case your truck gets stranded, or your licensed staff member is unable to work.

During the hiring process, it is wise to discuss these varied job requirements with your applicants so that they understand what would be expected of them while working for you.

Management

Determining your food truck management system is the next step. If you will be present most or all the time as the primary operator of your truck, you will likely be filling the role of manager of your staff in addition to administrative and cooking responsibilities. If there are days when you will not be present—and we do strongly recommend that you take days off (again, no one wants burnout)—you should consider hiring a manager or actively training a staff member to take on that role.

Management positions come with more responsibility, and, as such, managers can expect to be paid more for their work. The odds are that you will pay your staff an hourly wage. It is important to consider not only the minimum wage requirements for your area but also offering a competitive rate to encourage applicants. When considering the cost of each employee to your business, you will also need to factor into this the tax requirements for your state or country. We will go into these in more depth in an upcoming chapter.

A manager can help relieve some of the stress of daily operations, enabling you to focus on other aspects of getting your business running smoothly. They might be responsible for opening and closing your truck, opening and monitoring your POS system, ordering from your suppliers, managing other staff, and promoting your brand in addition to the standard food preparation and ordering roles often shared by everyone working in the truck at any one time. Not to mention, their most important role will be in communicating with you. It can be challenging to find someone you trust with this much responsibility, especially given the time, effort, and funds you invested into your business. Take your time interviewing for this position.

Do not be afraid to fill this role yourself, if possible, while looking for another manager. Working with your staff may also give you a sense of who might be ready and willing to take on additional responsibilities and whom you could promote. A bonus to this approach is that this staff member is already familiar with your food truck operation.

Wages and Benefits

You will need to work out the best scheduling approach for your truck, but bear in mind that there are legal restrictions on how you can schedule your employee's shifts. The same is true of wages and benefits. Much of this depends on how you can scale your food truck business. In the United States, you may opt to pay your staff as 1099 independent contractors, but most are hired as W-2 employees paid an hourly wage. There are significant penalties for claiming a full-time employee as a 1099 contractor, so be sure you understand the applicable tax code.

If you want to clarify which category your staff falls into, you can submit a free SS-8 form to the U.S. Internal Revenue Service. We will delve into taxes further in the chapter addressing legal considerations. You may even offer a competitive salary to a professional chef or experienced manager. Offering even basic benefits can also increase your staff retention and reduce the pressure and costs involved in hiring and training new employees. You will need to crunch your numbers to determine what your truck can support based on its current profit margins.

If you are interested in hiring someone, check their references and submit a background check request to confirm the accuracy of their resume. In the United States, programs like Background Info USA offer access to comprehensive criminal background checks. This is all the more important if your employee will be driving your food truck or working as front-of-house because insurers will run similar checks to determine premium costs and because food truck customers are often children.

Again, how you arrange your staff is entirely at your discretion. Remember that your staff represents your brand every time they work for you. You should communicate with them and support them with appropriate training that gives them the confidence and familiarity with your brand to communicate it effectively to your customers.

Human Resources

Set aside some time to compose an employee handbook. You can start from a template but focus on setting clear policies specific to your food truck in writing. When you have decided to hire someone, you can read through this handbook together and have your new hire sign a basic form acknowledging that they have read and understood what is expected of them. This initial conversation also gives you a platform to discuss the differences between the front and back-of-house staff with your new hires and make it clear which role they will be filling or whether they will be expected to do both.

Why is this important? Establishing these expectations for conduct and communication makes your life easier when you need to have a corrective conversation with an employee. A handbook also gives you an established way to include legally required policy information, such as a nondiscrimination policy, that will protect both you and your employees. It is also important to present a clear picture of the compensation, benefits, and guidelines for termination that you will follow. Your handbook is also an excellent means of introducing employees to the steps of their training.

Set yourself up for successful navigation of human resources by establishing clear guidelines that support the vision you have for your food truck. Document performance issues based on failure to meet standards established by your employee handbook. You will be able to more easily pinpoint and address failures to meet these expectations and protect your business from potential litigation.

These handbooks do not need to be professionally printed, but you should be able to give a physical copy to each member of your staff. Your handbook will need to be updated periodically as your business grows or government policies change.

Training

Daily Operations

As you begin to hire people to work as part of your food truck team, you want to give them the best chance of succeeding and working smoothly together. This will result in the best support for your vision for your food truck, and your customers will feel the impact of a happy and satisfied staff. As you iron out the details of day-to-day operations, we recommend composing a procedural guidebook that can be used as a training reference. In this guide, you will lay out the standards for each aspect of operating your food truck in detail. As your business grows, keep this document updated. Trust us, this small investment of time now will be worth it later.

With your first employees, you will be training directly. Over time, you may pass this responsibility on to a manager. The standards you set in your initial training are what your entire staff will base their own professional behavior and choices on, so make it count. Consider beforehand how you want to approach training. Do you want to use a classroom setting or assign some reading? Do you want to have training sessions in the truck but without customers? Do you want to have your trainee shadow you for several days? Most likely, a combination of these approaches will provide your new employees with the best chance to absorb and retain everything there is to know about running your food truck. Your approach will also depend upon how many new hires you are training together.

It might also make sense to focus on one aspect of your truck operation for each day of training. For example, you might emphasize cleanliness and safety best practices on one day, food preparation, storage, and cooking on the next day, customer service the following day, and finish up with operating the food truck. Work out an approach that makes the most sense for your truck and your employees, and remember that their training should be paid time. They are learning valuable skills that will enable them to support your business. When you do your job well, they will understand your expectations. This will also make your job easier when you find it necessary to redirect an employee back to these initially established standards.

Do not forget to give your trainees a break! People tend to retain information best in 20-minute increments, so consider some ways to break up your training sessions into manageable segments. Running a small business is stressful but do your best not to pass this stress on to your staff. They will perform better if they enjoy their work. This does not mean you should not maintain high standards of performance, only that creating a positive culture within your truck starts with you. In fact, this communal attitude will circle back around and make your time at work more fun, too. You started your food truck business because you have a passion for it; share that passion with your staff. We promise that positive work culture is contagious in the best way!

Customer Service

You might give your employees time to adjust to their new positions, or you might prefer to let them learn by doing. Whatever your approach, be certain you are providing them with enough information and skills to feel equipped for the tasks their job requires of them. People have different learning styles, and some may take longer to pick up on certain skills than others. Be patient. The more you invest in each employee, the better the outcomes will be. The best example of this is customer service.

The chances are good that you hired people who work well with others and are friendly and engaging, but customer service from a food truck may feel foreign even to people familiar with a food service environment. Consider that your front-of-house truck staff will be visible from the moment a customer approaches until they step away with their food. That can feel like a lot of pressure, especially in a high-speed environment.

Many free training videos are available online to walk your staff through the basics of customer service. Even for experienced staff, it does not hurt to have a refresher. They will pick up on your tone and attitude. If you make your customers and their experience a priority, so will your staff. Give them some basic language guidelines and phrases they can fall back on if they feel uncomfortable. Let them know you support them and when a customer's behavior should be addressed or brought to you or a manager's attention. Give them plenty of practice with your POS system so that they feel comfortable engaging with your customers while simultaneously entering and processing orders. It may help to assign a new staff member to a single task at first, rather than immediately requiring the multitasking that will be an essential part of their job on the truck.

In any small business, it is important to communicate with your employees. Since your staff will be performing multiple roles, make certain to let them know how you would like them to prioritize. You should also consider what you are willing to offer customers when you have made a mistake with their order. You should plan the best ways to document these incidents, too, so that you have a record in the event of any later need to follow up or even lawsuits. It may help to detail your customer service approach in your employee guidebook.

It often helps to frame your training approach from a team perspective. Each of the requirements you make of an employee should be backed by sound reasoning for how it supports your entire team. If this sounds unnecessary, just consider a time when you were asked to do something that seemed unnecessary. Your immediate response was likely resentment at being singled out or dismissal of the importance of the task. It helps people to understand the reasons behind their actions. Even something as simple as wearing your food truck's branded shirt or sanitizing a surface every time is easier to remember when your staff member knows why such a task is performed. Consider how you would explain the necessity of either of those behaviors. See? You are going to be a great trainer.

Food Service Training

Though we will cover the specifics of food safety certification in the next chapter, it is important to train your employees in safe food handling practices. Even if your city does not require every employee to obtain a permit, it is worth considering your customers and the product you are giving them. You want your customers to not only enjoy their food but trust it is safely prepared. Put bluntly: if your food makes someone sick, they are unlikely to buy from your truck again, much less recommend you to their friends.

Do some research into available video training courses that can take your employees through the basics of food handling safety. This will reduce risk to them, you, and your customers. Many of these educational courses are available for free, and you can find one that you like the best (some are, we admit, very cheesy). After viewing these videos, it helps to reinforce the recommended practices with some practical application. Practice safe knife usage and replacing your plastic gloves after cutting meat, for example. The extra work now will help keep your team working well together, too. If everyone is expecting the same standards of each other, you reduce the odds of misunderstandings and frustration surrounding these daily tasks and can focus on what matters: providing a great product to your customers.

Fire and Equipment Safety

While some cities include equipment inspections as part of their permit process, most do not require employees to complete fire safety training. Whether or not you include a fire safety course in your orientation of new employees, it is wise to have an emergency plan prepared. Discuss this plan with your staff so that everyone knows the appropriate procedure in the event of a fire or other equipment failure. Some food trucks use propane to fuel appliances, and there are specific fire and propane safety courses that cater to food trucks. We strongly recommend getting your entire staff on the same page regarding emergency procedures, and one of the simplest ways to manage this is to have everyone complete one of these training courses.

It is also smart to consider the functions specific to your truck and create an action plan in the event that various mechanisms or equipment malfunction. We will discuss the specifics involved in vehicle and road safety in the coming chapters.

Workplace Sensitivity Training

Though also not required by law in most cities, it is worth considering including sensitivity or similar training as part of your orientation process. This may be something you decide is necessary later, after your team has worked together for a while, but in general, it is good practice to establish these professional behavioral standards from the outset. There are many training courses, both free and paid, available online if you decide to go this route.

Chapter 6: Permits, Licenses, and Certifications

City codes, regulations, and training requirements for you and your staff will vary based on your location and even, to some extent, your planned hours and days of operation. Whether or not your city requires all the following types of training, we recommend investing in the safety of your hired employees and customers by providing some form of training. Foodborne illnesses can present a serious risk to people's health. In a food truck, you may be required to work closely with materials that pose a significant fire or injury risk if mishandled. Moreover, driving and parking an oversize vehicle such as a food truck, particularly on narrow, busy city streets, is another challenge altogether. Think through which employees will be performing which tasks, but consider requiring that all your employees have working knowledge and certification in all areas of food truck operation. This will give you scheduling flexibility and cut down on the number of days you are unable to be open for business. Ensuring that your entire business retains its insurance coverage can also depend upon maintaining updated certifications.

Above these liability concerns, however, thorough training can equip you and your staff to better serve your customers by setting shared standards and encouraging the development of healthy work culture. In the close quarters of a food truck, cleanliness and safety procedures involving food and equipment are especially important. You will reduce the stress around health inspections if your truck is maintained at a high standard of cleanliness all the time, and your employees will be happier to work in the close confines of a well-maintained truck than a dirty or potentially dangerous one.

Food Safety Certification

Certification requirements vary dramatically from country to country, but generally, these standards are set at the national level and enforced at the local level. That is, your country's equivalent of the Food and Drug Administration (FDA) may set quality standards for all food products or services, but you and your employee's certification will be processed through a local health department. In the United States, each different jurisdiction has different food safety training requirements, too. Though all state requirements meet the federal standards, some include additional requirements based on how food service and sales are regulated at the state level. Some health departments require that you keep your food handler card on you at any time you are preparing or serving food. Others require a food protection manager certification.

The National Registry offers a state-by-state guide that outlines which certifications are required and by whom. The current Centers for Disease Control recommendation is to have at least one certified food protection manager on-site to reduce the risk of a foodborne illness outbreak. But here, too, the actual requirements differ. It is crucial to do your research to find out the exact requirements for the areas where your truck will be serving food.

In certain states, food handler safety certification is voluntary rather than required. For example, the Food Code in the state of Missouri only requires that the individual in charge of daily operations demonstrate knowledge of the food safety principles collectively known as HACCP (Hazard Analysis and Critical Control Point). The state's government website provides links to relevant food safety training programs, which can be completed online. A similar process is necessary to acquire a license to sell liquor in Missouri. In fact, in Missouri, all food certifications and training can be taken online, after which you must appear in person with your driver's license or other proof of identification and pay a fee to receive your certification card. It is a clever idea to check your local regulatory body's website to determine what food safety training is required of you and of your staff. Some states require the certificate applicant to appear in person, while some allow you to pay for your permit online. These sites will also contain licensing and regulatory information you should be aware of as a food truck business owner.

Often, multiple food safety certifications are required to legally operate your business. That said, even if not, these courses are empowering and are practical tools that increase relevant workplace skill sets and knowledge. It is wise to get a jump start on completing your staff's training. We recommend having your newly hired staff members complete the relevant online training as part of their orientation. Including an updated list of certifications in your employee handbook is an excellent resource as well.

Vehicle Operation

As we will discuss in the upcoming chapters, some food trucks are, in fact, trailers. These trailers are connected to trucks or other vehicles with the capacity to haul them from location to location, where they are parked, disconnected, and set up for food service. In such cases, you may only need a standard driver's license issued by your state government to transport your food truck trailer. Many self-contained food trucks are also small enough to meet standard licensing requirements. But it is important to check the requirements for your state since some states use vehicle length and weight to determine eligibility and permits.

As you have probably considered, you may need to apply for and obtain a commercial driver's license to drive your food truck between locations. Certain regions also distinguish between commercial truck driving and food truck driving within the licensing system. While it is essential for you to obtain the appropriate licensing, it is a good idea to ensure that at least one other person present is also licensed to operate your food truck at any given time. Preparing for the unexpected is a great way to keep your truck operating for as many hours as possible within the limitations imposed by your local government and the weather. Backup systems are important, and we recommend working towards having some form of backup established for all of the vital parts of your food truck business.

Costs differ slightly for driver's licenses in different states, with commercial licenses generally running at around $100. Your local DMV (Department of Motor Vehicles) website will have the information you need regarding whether you should apply for a commercial driver's license and what steps you will need to take to complete your application. You may need to complete an online course or in-person test. Some places even require a certain number of driving hours before your driving permit is advanced into a full and unlimited license. If you are the primary driver of the food truck, it may also be worth investing in a defensive driving course for your own peace of mind. As a bonus, such training can also reduce your insurance premiums.

We know that, by now, it probably seems that every step of building your food truck business requires some research into local regulations and requirements, but it will be worth putting in this effort now to prevent entanglements later!

Business Licensing

In general terms, your city, county, or state regulatory body will require you to obtain a basic business operation license or vendor license, which, essentially, permits you to operate your food truck in that location as a recognized business. This registration will also be important when filing your taxes. You must pay to receive the appropriate licensing, and the cost varies by location, up to around $500. Just like standard car registration, your business license is also subject to renewal. You should keep track of when to renew your license and budget for this expense. It is a good idea to set up a business calendar application that will prompt you when such expenses are upcoming. It can be easier to be caught by surprise by annual or semi-annual charges since they are not part of your standard monthly expenses.

Certain cities impose limits on mobile vendors like food trucks, either capping the total allowable number of vendors within city limits or placing restrictions on the times, days of the week, or certain seasonal or holiday dates when they may operate. Some cities use a lottery system that you must submit to each year or which you must enter as a new vendor until a slot opens. These systems can be quite competitive, which is another reason to make certain that your truck remains operational by completing and maintaining all your registrations and permits. You do not want to lose your access because of something so comparatively insignificant.

Check your local requirements to get your applications in as early as possible. Generally, you do not have to own an operational truck to begin this process, which can take some time and might be competitive. In the United States, the SBA (Small Business Administration) runs a website that will provide you with the details of licensing requirements in your city.

Government Identification Number

When you register your business with your federal government, you will be given a unique identifying number. In the United States, this number is issued by the IRS (Internal Revenue Service). Each country has a similar regulatory body that allows the government to track and appropriately tax your business. Your number generates an electronic record of all your business information and keeps track of your tax status, federal licensing, and any other relevant data. Be aware that, while the process is free, it may take up to several months to receive your EIN after submitting your application. Apply early!

Food Handler Permits

As discussed in a previous chapter, food safety training requirements vary by city. Health inspectors will enforce your area regulations, so be sure you understand and are meeting those requirements before scheduling your inspection. Generally, a manager or the entire staff will be required to carry a valid permit whenever food is being prepared. In some areas, you may need to visibly post your permits. Most businesses keep copies of their employee's permits on file in the event that they are lost or to keep track of when they need to be recertified. Depending on local requirements, permitting may require studying provided material and passing a test.

Fortunately, these permits are usually less expensive to obtain, running up to around $50 and sometimes as low as $10. If your employees are required to obtain permits, remember to have them keep track of time spent doing so and compensate them appropriately, as this task is a work requirement and not voluntary.

Food Service Licensing

Your health department will issue your food truck this permit once it passes a health inspection. When building your truck and establishing operational standards, make sure you consult your local health code to ensure you are meeting these requirements. This generally involves cleanliness, appropriate food storage, and posted HACCP or comparable plans. The specific arrangements for your truck will need to be worked out based on the demands of your unique cuisine and preferences. For example, you may need to store your fire extinguisher a certain distance away from open flame or heat sources. In the confines of a food truck, organizing equipment to maintain compatibility with health codes can be a challenge. The more work you complete in advance of installing your equipment, the less you will need to deal with the hassle of reorganization or even rebuilding.

Like all food service establishments, your truck will be given a health grade that must be visible to customers. The visibility requirement, too, varies by location. Your local health department may require that your grade be posted on the outside of your food truck, at eye level, or beside your menu. Or it may simply require that you post your grade within the eye line of your customers as they look through the customer service window to the inside of your truck. In whatever way it must be displayed, your grade must be on your truck at all times when it is in operation.

Though this may seem like yet another hoop to jump through and a hassle to complete, a positive inspection can actually work in your favor. The higher your grade, the more confidence your customers will have in your product. When you are ready for your inspection, you can schedule an appointment with your local health department. Food service permits fall at the more expensive end of the licensing spectrum, up to $1000, and will need to be renewed. Since this is one of the requirements for keeping your truck operational, be sure to educate yourself about your health code and keep your food service license current.

Operating a food truck without a license can result in more than just significant fines. You may have your business license revoked or be banned from operating as a vendor in your region. We are not trying to add to what we know is likely a lot of anxiety surrounding the intensive permitting process; however, it is important to be aware of the repercussions of failing to meet regulations or allowing your permits to expire.

A responsible business owner will ensure that someone, either owner or an employee, works as a dedicated back-of-house staff member, keeping track of not only the books but also all the relevant permits and certifications. This approach will help keep you from letting any essential components or steps slip through the cracks.

Miscellaneous

While most cities require some version of all the above, the need for the following permits and certifications varies by city:

- Certain locations require business owners in food service to obtain a seller's permit to avoid paying sales tax on wholesale items that their customers will end up paying. In the United States, if you are located near a state line and will be serving food in several states, be sure you understand how sales tax requirements differ between states.

- Some places require your truck to be certified by the local fire department as well as the health department. In such cases, you may need to keep appropriate fire suppression equipment on hand and maintain cooking equipment to predetermined standards. Including regularly having your propane tanks and fire extinguisher inspected. In general, these are best practices for any food truck, though you will need to research specifically applicable code. In some places, your fire suppression equipment will be part of your health department inspection.

- It may seem obvious, but most cities require parking permits for food trucks, with certain locations permanently off-limits to vendors. They may also specify whether your truck must be garaged overnight and limit the permitted hours of operation. In some areas, you may have the option to pay an additional fee to operate overnight or during certain seasons. In general, and particularly in larger cities, parking permits can be expensive since most areas charge a daily rate. You must factor this expense into your monthly budget, which also means planning how many days you will be open. Street vendors may have special access to monthly or annual parking permits, but you will need to go to your city government's website for more information specific to your situation.

- As we have discussed, you may choose to prepare some or all the ingredients for your meals in advance in a commercial-grade kitchen. In some cities, this is not an option but a requirement. In these locations, you will need to store and prepare your food in what is known as a commissary kitchen, an arrangement that includes a signed letter from the facility granting you and your staff access to the appliances and utilities. In general, this is to ensure that proper food safety measures are being followed and to guarantee that all vendors have unbroken access to food storage maintained at safe temperatures.

- In a few highly regulated locations, the city might require you to submit a document detailing your standard operating procedures. Cities which rely heavily on tourism or which are built in areas with significant environmental protection policies in place are likely to fall into this category. While not required by most locations, such a document is a useful reference tool for training new employees and is worth composing as a business document. It generally includes step-by-step procedures for everything from basic employee tasks within the truck to meal preparation and how the truck is locked and stored overnight. We recommend composing a standard operations document, especially if you plan to expand and will need to be certain to maintain quality and service standards across multiple trucks or locations.

- Once your food truck is up and running, you will likely begin to take on catering jobs, festivals, or work at what are known inclusively as special events. Your city will require a permit, usually for a fee, granting your food truck temporary access to whatever venue or facility is hosting the event. Generally, permit applications can be submitted online, but processing times vary, so be sure to leave enough time before your event. Such events may also require the purchase of additional parking passes for personal vehicles or your food truck.

As you can tell, it is important to factor in business licensing fees when projecting overhead expenses for your food truck. These fees will quickly add up to a significant amount and, depending on your city, can even put your rollout plan on hold as you wait for an application to be processed.

We recommend creating a complete list of all the permits, licenses, and certifications required for food trucks in your city, even if they do not currently apply to your truck. For example, there may be restricted parking hours on streets in another neighborhood. Though you may not plan to operate at that location, you may end up catering in that area or discover that it offers particularly good access to foot traffic on certain days. Having this information ready to hand can help you prepare well and serve as a reminder to check every relevant permitting consideration for a new location. Overall, this reference list will be a useful resource and a good way to double-check that your current certifications are all valid, too.

Chapter 7: Building Your Truck

Outfitting your truck to the appropriate specifications is more than acquiring a truck and having your brand-appropriate vinyl wrap applied. Before you apply for a microloan or begin crowdfunding for the funds to purchase your truck, you will need to decide the size and type of food truck that best matches your location, travel, and food preparation demands. Some of this may depend on the regulations in your area and health code requirements, but the food truck equipment you will need will depend on the type of cuisine you plan to serve and how much cooking and assembly will occur in the truck. For instance, deep fryers must be set up to meet specific safety standards, and refrigerators must have the capacity to maintain safe food temperatures reliably.

You must also consider how to source all these truck components. Though you may have lower insurance premiums on new equipment, investments of over $500 are generally eligible for depreciation tax deductions, whether or not you purchase them new. Essentially, this means that you are able to stretch your tax benefits out over time rather than taking a single lump deduction. If you are financially able to pay slightly more in your first year, the depreciation approach can, in fact, save you more over time.

Of course, when considering equipment purchases, you will need to balance your budget demands against your need for efficiency within your truck, food safety, and final product quality. When shopping for your equipment, remember that these items will not be sitting stationary in a restaurant but be moved around and used in a confined space. Here, every inch of space and ounce of weight counts. For this reason, you will be looking for primarily food truck-specific appliances, though smaller repurposed restaurant equipment may be an option as well. Much of this will depend on what is necessary to complete your unique meals.

Keep in mind that the less prep and cooking you must do in the truck, the quicker your meal turnaround and the more customers you can serve. That said, part of the appeal of your truck may be in its grilled-to-order offerings or freshly cut fruit toppings. You will need to work out a balance between the quality you want to deliver to your customers and the practicalities of serving out of a food truck. In fact, this may be something that you need to edit later. The good thing about sourcing the kinds of commercial-grade equipment you will be investing in is that they are relatively easy to sell back, assuming you have maintained a decent maintenance and cleaning routine. So, if you do decide to make a change, do not be afraid to go for it.

Essentially, the value to you of a completely outfitted truck will depend on the type of foods you plan to prepare. If you do not require specialized equipment, it may make the most sense to purchase a truck that already includes the basic elements you will need and make any minor alterations yourself. Though we have mentioned mostly cooking equipment so far, consider that your truck will also need to be able to maintain cleanliness throughout a shift. You will need a deep commercial sink with three wells and a separate handwashing sink to keep to code. You may also consider a sanitizing and drying dishwasher, though this would draw so much power that it would be a significant investment. If you decide to look for a truck that is already outfitted with the basic equipment, these are all choices you will need to make. Consider the extra effort and staff hours that might go into washing dishes against the expense of a sanitizing dishwasher, both upfront and as it draws on utilities.

However, in many cases, it will be less expensive to source your truck and commercial equipment components separately, even with the additional cost of installation. Why is this? In part, when you purchase pieces of equipment individually, you can seek out and use different sellers to get a better value on refurbished or new components that may be significantly older than your truck or vice versa. In this way, you can hunt down deals and make the most of financing options for each of the major kitchen appliances you will be using.

You will also need to decide between power options for all this equipment: electric, propane, or gas, or some combination of the three. A single electric generator is often not enough to keep up with the power demands of a food truck, so you may even need two, and generators are not cheap. However, if precise temperatures are important to your cuisine and you will be relying heavily on an oven, electric power is likely a wise choice. For high-temperature cooking, gas is a much more efficient option. However, flammable gas is also the most potentially dangerous of all the power options within the small confines of a small truck. Gas is also much easier to access and the least expensive option. Propane gas is even more heat-efficient and, especially if you are aiming for a more environmentally friendly truck, a good choice. However, it is more expensive than gas.

Depending on your plans for the truck, you may even want to invest in slightly more expensive dual-option gas appliances that can be used with gas or propane. If you plan to split your time between street service and festivals, for instance, this might be an approach to consider. You will need to consider your access to fuel for your truck, as well as whether you want to invest in a generator or opt for the more portable propane or less expensive gas to power your equipment.

A good food truck business owner is a creative problem solver or quickly becomes one. If this is not one of your strengths, you may even consider bringing in a partner to share some of the burden and risk of starting up a small business. However you make it happen, building your physical truck requires a lot of effort but can also be incredibly rewarding. For the first time, you will have a physical manifestation of what, until now, has only been an intangible concept in your head. Now, on to the specifics!

Truck or Trailer?

Several factors play into the choice between a food truck and a trailer. First, be sure to check the regulations for your city to confirm whether both are viable options. Parking restrictions and food preparation requirements, in particular, may impact your decision. Most health and fire safety requirements can be met in either a truck or trailer, so the biggest factors involved in this decision will be mobility and space.

In general, food trailers cost much less upfront than a complete food truck. They also offer more storage space and larger windows, expanding your options and the number of customers you may be able to serve. This is because they do not need to account for cab or engine space. They also offer the benefit of being able to use multiple different vehicles for towing if your primary vehicle ever requires maintenance. Over time, a vehicle towing a trailer will get slightly better mileage than a food truck, so trailers tend to be the preferred option for food truck businesses that will do a significant amount of traveling. However, a trailer requires a vehicle with an appropriate hitch and towing capacity.

That said, food trucks are more mobile than trailers overall since trailers require much longer to set up and break down and do not have the same maneuverability. Trailers are not a great option if you plan to relocate your truck during your workday to capitalize on customer traffic. You will also need registration and insurance to cover both your towing vehicle and trailer. Food trucks require less time to set up after reaching their destination and do not require additional accommodations to be made for a towing vehicle. In some ways, food trailers can also offer more comfort to customers since they have room to include tables and chairs that can be set up on location. They are a good choice for areas with more space where relocation is not necessary during the day, like special events and festivals.

Both trailers and trucks can be effective means of supplementing existing restaurant income, so this will factor less into your choice. This decision comes down to the food you plan to serve and where you plan to serve it, at least as a primary location. It also depends in part on your financial capacity. If you already own a vehicle with the appropriate towing capacity, renting or buying a trailer may even serve as a means of earning enough to ultimately purchase a food truck. Carefully consider which of these factors will have the greatest impact on your food truck business. Now, you can begin looking for your new (or gently used) food truck or trailer!

Industrial Suppliers

Having made the decision between truck or trailer, you can begin to consider outfitting your chosen vehicle with the necessary appliances to cook your custom food. As we discussed in previous chapters, large appliances are often available for reasonable financing deals. Depending on what type of food you will be selling, you may require a grill, oven, stovetop, large capacity refrigerator or freezer, extra sinks, even a nitrogen tank, or other more specialized equipment, like a high-yield waffle maker, popcorn machine, or custom fryer. The equation becomes more complicated by the fact that you must fit all these elements inside your food truck in a way that allows you and your employees to rush around preparing your food.

Though we discussed the importance of saving space, it is important to devote that space to the heart of your food truck as needed. For most trucks, this will be your stovetop or grill. Though it seems almost trivial, consider how important having those extra burners will be when you are at peak hours. We recommend working out, based on the length of time it takes to prepare a meal, the size of the cooking surface that can maximize your efficiency. At a certain point, extra burners will provide no added benefit. The best way to test this may be to use a test or commissary kitchen to determine how your order-to-completion time and order capacity will rely on your cooking space. In general, or if you are unable to work out exactly what you think you might need, four burners are a good place to start. It should be noted here that regulations in some areas require sprinklers to be installed as part of a food truck's fire suppression system, depending on what equipment is being used. Flat-top griddles, in particular, may require sprinklers.

You will have options for temperature control, from basic to incredibly accurate, for all your heating and cooling equipment. It is worth paying attention to whether or not you will be able to store items on top of different appliances, like a freezer or refrigerator, and what the weight limits are. Remember, space is at a premium.

As far as where to begin looking to get a sense of price points and to simply explore what all your options might be, used and new equipment is available online through numerous restaurant resellers such as Burkett, Gator Chef, Restaurant Equippers, and Cullincini. Even Facebook marketplace, eBay, and Craigslist are great options for smaller equipment. You should also look into local auctions and online auction sites, like Bid On Equipment. In the United States, there is even a government-run auction site for the resale of surplus equipment from various agencies called GOV Deals. When you inevitably get some sticker shock at the prices of your equipment, remember the purpose each item serves within your truck and the value it is adding.

Once your commercial equipment is purchased and installed, you will need to check your truck for many of the smaller but essential safety features. For example, your cabinet doors will all require locks, not only as theft deterrents but to prevent them from opening during travel. There will be many safety elements to consider when composing your truck, but it is not only here that practical considerations come into play. While we encourage you to begin to build your brand around your custom food offering, you should consider this concept flexible. What do we mean? Simply that you may discover a fantastic offer on a truck much smaller than you originally planned for. This might mean adjusting your overall approach by reducing the size of your menu and capitalizing on the opportunity to reallocate the saved money toward marketing or quality ingredients. Every step of the way, you will be confronted with new challenges.

There are companies that can customize your food truck kitchen to your specifications. This includes outfitting your truck with all the cabinets and shelves you need, as well as any extra vents or fans, display fixtures, lights, collapsible awnings, electrical wiring, and outlets. If you can imagine it, there is some company out there that can make it for you. These companies will be able to take your ideas and provide guidance and quotes. These custom jobs may not be cheap, but they are an investment in the future success of your food truck. For every decision you make, remember that you will be spending long hours in this limited space with your staff.

Maintenance

Keeping track of and performing routine maintenance on your truck will extend its life and help prevent costly breakdowns. Should you decide to resell your truck, these records will also provide evidence of its value. Whether your engine is in your truck or the vehicle you use to tow your food trailer, it will benefit from regular oil changes and system checks. Find a garage you can rely on; you may be able to make an arrangement or special deal for using their services exclusively. Alongside these regular costs are the costs of gas to fuel your truck. Together, these costs average between $500 and $1000 each month.

Your generator will also need regular maintenance. You will need to consider batter replacements, as well as maintaining any gas systems to a high safety standard. There are areas where you can consider cutting costs: safety should never be one of them. Though inspections will point out any major issues, you should not wait for something to break down or fail to meet the quality code. All your heating elements pose a significant fire risk if not properly cleaned and maintained.

Maintenance involves more than engine and equipment care, of course. Be sure to add routine cleanings of your truck kitchen to your business calendar. The interior of your truck will be exposed to outdoor air often enough that it will accumulate more dust than you might expect. In fact, one of the best features of a food truck is that, unlike a restaurant, it can be power-washed, inside and out. This is one of the insider tips any food truck owner who has been in the business for long will tell you. Rather than waste time and effort doing your initial wipe-downs at the end of the day, invest in a power washer or find a local car wash where you can rent or pay for the use of one. This will save you hours and allow you to skip to the important sanitization of food preparation surfaces, and save your effort for other cleanings of hard-to-reach areas.

The floor of your food truck should not be overlooked in this process. In fact, keeping your food truck floors clean can prevent serious injury to your employees. We recommend removable commercial mats. The floor of your truck will, inevitably, get slick and could pose a serious risk. Restaurant kitchen mats are a great option since they can be easily removed for cleaning and even cut to custom fit your truck.

In addition to removing oil or other residues from your exhaust hood and appliances, be sure to dust lights and disinfect your cooling units. Not only will this help you meet code and safety requirements, but regular cleaning will reduce breakdowns and also extend the life of your appliances, keeping your truck running longer. Even elements as simple as ensuring lightbulbs are replaced promptly can you're your food truck kitchen operating as safely as possible. All of these little elements could be easy to let slide. Committing now to maintaining a high standard of safety and cleanliness in your truck will help prompt you to take the time to address those pesky maintenance concerns as they arise, rather than letting them build into a dangerous problem.

Moreover, care of your truck and commercial equipment can reduce your insurance premiums, no small matter when covering liability for a mobile food service operation.

You probably have some sense of the average cost of car insurance for a personal vehicle, and it is not insignificant. Consider that your truck is also your business. It is where your employees operate and how customers access your food. Given all the hard-working components of your truck, it makes sense to care for each one and keep it running smoothly. You will have enough stress without adding repair costs. We will discuss insurance in depth soon, but for now, consider that even individual pieces of equipment can be separately insured. Your commercial-grade kitchen equipment and truck are your business; without them, your small business is just a dream.

Why are we emphasizing this point? It can be easy to let small cleaning or routine maintenance tasks fall by the wayside when you are busy and exhausted. It might be worth brainstorming some strategies that will work for you to help keep you accountable to yourself for these important elements. Whatever works best for you, we recommend acting on this strategy now so that, when your future self is worn out and riding the high of a huge sales day and just wants to skip the deep clean for a day, you will choose to not let your workday be over until your food truck is fully cleaned and prepared for the next great sales day.

Chapter 8: The Legal Side

As you might expect, this chapter will likely not be anyone's favorite. Intellectual property rights, tax law, and insurance coverage are very few people's ideas of a good time. However, these hurdles are necessary to get you to your goal of food truck business ownership, and with this book, we are committed to making that process as painless as possible. While much of the relevant legal issues will be specific to your location, there are general areas in which preparation can help you avoid being blindsided by penalty fees or becoming entangled in litigation.

Intellectual Property

From your concept to your recipes, your food truck business is your creation. It makes sense that you will want to protect it from physical theft, but what about the idea itself? Essentially, that is what we are discussing when we talk about intellectual property. To begin to protect your rights to your idea and concept, the best thing you can do is to pursue a trademark. When pursuing a trademark of your name and logo in the United States, the Patent and Trademark Office (USPTO) is the best place to start.

First, you can use the national database to confirm that no existing company has a prior trademark in place on a similar name. You should conduct an internet search to confirm that no existing company in your area has a prior claim to the name. However, even if they have not registered a trademark, a business may have rights to a name through United States common law. Most countries have similar protections in place for the first user of a name. It is wise to confirm that you will not be raising any rights disputes by performing some simple searches. Then, you can confirm that your brand name and logo are unique enough to qualify for a trademark.

For the most part, as a food truck business owner, you will not need to be overly concerned with anyone attempting to use your brand until you acquire a larger following, so this is one aspect of your food truck business that can wait. It is also an involved process that takes a significant time commitment, so do not think you need to rush to acquire a trademark during your first year.

It may also be worth employing or at least consulting with an attorney when pursuing intellectual property registration. Flat-fee subscriptions to LegalZoom or similar legal service operations offer small businesses many forms of legal support and are worth considering. Most are quite affordable and only require setting up phone consultations or meetings in advance. These legal service providers can help you review more than just your intellectual property rights, however. They can also confirm that you are covered against liability in all aspects of your business, from insurance to permits. As you are starting out with a food truck, this is advisable since there are so many aspects of food truck operation that involve potential financial penalties. In fact, LegalZoom has specific options for assisting in trademark registration.

Copyright, on the other hand, involves the right to publish and sell your creative work. For a food truck business, this can include promotional materials and your menu. A proprietary recipe or food formula is considered your intellectual property and can be similarly protected. If you do decide to register a "secret sauce," you should also have an NDA, or non-disclosure agreement, prepared for your staff and keep your formula and its preparation out of sight. While it is wise to have these protections in place, if you do ever realize your work is being copied or reproduced without your consent, it is worth consulting a legal specialist about how best to approach enforcing your copyright.

If you live outside of the United States, your government's website or offices should be able to direct you to the relevant law and registration options. As a bonus, if you are ever interested in reselling your business, having trademarks and copyrights in place provides additional evidence of value.

Taxes

No one enjoys taxes, but as a small business owner, you cannot afford not to take your tax obligations seriously. We recommend hiring a professional if this is something your budget can accommodate. Even if you do hire a tax professional, it is smart to be aware of the many relevant aspects of tax law. In this book, we delve into relevant law within the United States. For food truck businesses operating in other countries, the same general advice applies. That is, we recommend hiring a tax professional who knows what they are doing and can ensure you are not missing any documentation that might leave you vulnerable or subject to costly penalties.

All of this is complicated by the mobility of your truck, especially if you live near a state border or travel out of state for festivals or other events. You will need to be careful to plan for different sales tax percentages in the way that you plan for different parking permits and any other differences in regulations.

Local Sales Tax

There are several aspects of taxation you should be aware of as a food truck business owner. The first is sales tax. In the United States, these taxes vary by state, but you may need to charge a sales tax to your customers that you then return to the state. To do this, you will need a sales tax permit. Generally, you are able to register for this permit through the state tax authority. Since these requirements vary state to state, we recommend determining what you will be required to charge well in advance of your intended opening since you will need to wait for registration confirmation before you can legally sell your food. Your POS software will enable you to input the percentage sales tax charged on each order.

State/Province Tax

As a small business owner, each year, you will be required to pay both state and federal income taxes. State taxes vary based on whether your business is registered as a sole proprietorship or LLC. In some states, you may be subject to an additional business income tax. The best way to determine what the applicable state tax requirements are for you is to search the website for that state's Department of Revenue.

Federal Business Tax

How you file your business taxes determines more than just the amounts you are responsible for paying. It also impacts whether your liability is separate from your business. The amount you must pay will depend on your profits, where you are operating, and your business entity classification. You can file several ways.

If you are starting small and do not have the time to commit to filing for incorporation, you may choose to register and run your business as a sole proprietor. However, this does not provide any financial separation from your business, and your personal assets are fair game if you face lawsuits or bankruptcy. Basically, you are self-employed, so you continue to file a personal 1040 with an added C and SE to include your business profits and losses. One downside to filing as a sole proprietor is that, depending on your revenue, you may need to pay estimated quarterly taxes. Essentially, this means that you will need to estimate your annual tax obligation and pay 25% of that amount each quarter of the fiscal year to avoid a penalty at the end of the year.

One of the more popular choices for food truck businesses is to form an LLC, a limited liability company. As the owner of a small food truck business, you can use an LLC to ensure that your personal assets are protected while allowing you to avoid the paperwork involved in registering a full corporation. In fact, filing as an LLC requires you to submit the same tax forms as a sole proprietorship.

Another method that gives you a certain amount of protection is to form a partnership to share the risk involved in running a small business. As a partnership business entity, you have many of the same protections as under an LLC, though you will need to fill out an additional 1065 tax form and have each partner submit a K-1. A business partnership is not something to be entered into lightly, and it is important not to equate your personal opinions of someone with their ability to be a good business partner. In a small business, connecting with your partner on a personal level is important because you will share so many decisions and must trust one another. However, your best friend may not be the best choice for a business partner. Be sure you understand how your potential partner handles responsibility, management, and money before you commit to beginning a business with them.

Though these are the most common approaches to food truck business ownership, you may find that as your business expands that you would be better suited by becoming an S or C Corporation. Both classifications involve shareholding in your business and result in dramatically more complicated tax filing requirements. This might occur if you bring in more trucks or brick-and-mortar locations and grow your number of employees. Generally, a good gauge of when it is time to incorporate is when you begin to require a level of management between you and your daily operations employees. Put simply, when your business needs managers, you are beginning to step up the rung of organizational complexity. This can be a great thing if it is what you want for your brand. However, it does come with added complications, so it is best to consult with a business advisor before deciding to alter your business registration status.

Deductions

Along with these various tax requirements, your small business will be able to benefit from deductions designed specifically to lift some of the weight from an emerging business. There are several, in particular, that you should pay close attention to as a food truck business owner. As we have established, your larger purchases will be for high-performing commercial equipment. For this reason, it is valuable to keep track of those purchases. In fact, for any equipment purchase over $500, the following deduction applies. You will have an option to claim a single, big deduction on these items when you first purchase them.

However, if you plan to operate your business for more than one or two years, you will likely benefit from depreciating these expenses across several years to maximize your tax benefit. We began to address this in a previous chapter, but essentially depreciation allows you to account for that significant investment of equipment across multiple years. This makes sense because this equipment is serving an essential function to your business for all these years. While a single lump tax break seems enticing, you will ultimately save more if you are able to file these expenses accounting for depreciation over time.

Travel is another area where you can make the most of deductions as a food truck operator. Even within a single city, you will drive your truck daily, even if only to and from its parking spot. Those miles and even half-miles add up. Depending on your brand and business model, you may cover hundreds of miles traveling to and from festivals. To make the most of the profit opportunities at festivals, you will accumulate lodging, meal, and fuel expenses for you and your employees. Keeping records of each of these transactions will allow you to deduct these expenses from your taxes as business expenses. You can even deduct any extra costs specific to each event, such as application fees, additional permits, and temporary hires. Like permit fees, these costs can seem individually small or insignificant, but together they add up to a sum worth accounting for.

Vehicle-specific deductions can be made in two different ways for food trucks. You can choose to deduct a standard mileage rate for the miles you travel or itemize expenses related to your food truck. It is generally difficult to know which option will result in a larger deduction, but for an itemized deduction, you must keep records of all relevant expenses. These include maintenance costs, like oil changes and fluid replacement, as well as parking and toll fees. Various phone applications help you track your mileage and other vehicle costs. It may make sense to track both options and wait to see which gives you the better deduction when you file. Since you will likely be tracking these expenses anyway, it is not much of a stretch to calculate which vehicle deduction makes the most sense for you in a given year. In fact, your choice of deduction may vary year to year, depending on changes in the amount of traveling you do or if you had major repair costs in a given year.

Insurance

As we have mentioned, owning a business comes with the weight of liability. Owning a food truck specifically, you will need to pay for multiple forms of insurance designed to cover you, your staff, and your business as an entity. Insurance requirements are set at the federal and local levels, and lenders often require that you submit proof of insurance before paying out a loan. Above the legal requirements, however, purchasing insurance for your business is a smart choice. You made a significant investment in your food truck business, and it is worth protecting. Insurance requirements vary by location, but some of the most common include:

- Commercial vehicle insurance: Like standard vehicle insurance, this will cover costs in the event of an accident. The cost to you depends on several factors, including your driver's license and accident history.

- General Liability: Before you can receive a commercial driver's license, you may need to prove you are covered for property damage or personal injuries that result from your business. Any other employees applying for a commercial license will also need to provide either this information or be able to reference you as an insured employer.

- Worker Compensation: As an employer, you will need to be insured to cover employee injury that might result in medical and legal costs in addition to lost income. This is a sound business decision and legal requirement, but also evidence of your respect for your employees.

- Property Insurance: With this coverage, you can protect specific high-price pieces of equipment against theft or damage. Your larger equipment and truck are valuable assets and vulnerable to theft, no matter what security measures you have in place. That said, your insurance premiums may be reduced by evidence of adequate security systems.

Depending on the type of insurance coverage you choose, these costs may be deductible from your business income taxes. Your best approach will likely be to consult with a tax professional who can advise you on your options and help you avoid filing errors. Yes, this is an additional expense, but it is a significantly lower expense than a penalty for underpayment. Working with a professional can also give you peace of mind about a complicated tax system. That said, the tax software we listed previously is a great place to start if you have the time to input your own financial business data.

In addition to these deduction categories, you will be able to deduct almost all the costs of running your business, including your inventory and supplies, as well as any commissary or other kitchen leasing or rental costs. While it can be time-consuming to keep track of all the little costs, they will accumulate over time and benefit your business in the long run. Eligible expenses include all food items, cooking dishes and utensils, paper products, marketing costs, commissary or comparable fees, employee wages and benefits, and training costs.

Many business insurance companies offer specific food truck insurance designed to protect your business and your customers. After consulting with a tax professional, it will probably make sense to get several quotes before deciding which insurance package best meets your needs.

Legislation

Though you will do the bulk of the work of ensuring that your business has met all its legal requirements for operation before your food truck opens, it is important to remember that legislation is subject to change. Mobile vendor regulations are volatile and regularly updated to account for the developing industry. This is another instance where membership in professional food truck organizations can provide you with a direct benefit, as these groups will often contact their members when applicable legislation is being proposed or passed. Remaining aware of the changing legal ground can help keep your business from getting fined or even temporarily suspended from operation.

Different ordinances apply based on your specific form of vending and location, so it is wise to remain aware of your city's regulations and check that any businesses you partner with are also meeting their legal requirements for operation. As in almost all aspects of your food truck business, the internet is your friend. It gives you access to updated legislation, but this requires that you utilize it well. It may be wise to schedule some time to check for new or pending laws applicable to your food truck business every month.

Other Considerations

Though we discussed permits and licensing in detail in an earlier chapter, it is worth reiterating here that acquiring the appropriate food truck permits and licensing is a complicated process that varies by location. You will likely be required to obtain multiple permits and become a documented business to legally operate your food truck. Your state government's website will direct you to the lists of required permits.

There are many other situational considerations to account for when planning to start a food truck business. In any country, your citizenship or resident status will impact your ability to obtain a business license. If you have a criminal history, this will also complicate the process and impact your ability to employ others. In the United States, specific regulations vary by state, but you can contact your licensing agency through their website or phone number to determine the specifics of your eligibility and whether you will need to submit to any additional evaluation.

None of this information is comprehensive. We are not giving legal or tax advice, only attempting to alert you to some of the steps you will need to take to become a legal mobile vendor and directing you to resources to ensure that you complete the necessary legal aspects of small business ownership.

Chapter 9: The Eats

At last, the chapter you have been waiting for! We know how important your food concept is; it may even be your original motivation for developing a food truck business. We hope to give you some guidelines in this chapter to help you convert your foody passion into a specific, actionable, and affordable menu plan that will work for you and your truck. Your general food concept is likely already decided, at least in part. Now, we will expand that concept into a practical and appealing menu.

However, it is also possible that your decision to start a food truck was more calculated by profit considerations, and you have yet to give much thought to your food or menu. If this is your situation, this chapter should provide a solid framework for developing a menu of which you can be proud (and which will keep your customers coming back again and again with their friends).

When working out a branding approach for your food truck, you considered how your central food item would play into and be supported by your brand. This may be something as simple as settling on a catchy name for your truck, applying a unifying theme, or deciding to embrace a regional cuisine. Whatever the case, your menu will be built on this foundational food concept, so if you have put it off, now is the time to decide!

If you are completely out of your element, we suggest getting together with some friends who enjoy restaurants or food in general. Visit some of the most popular, affordable restaurants in your area. Scope out the food truck scene, if any. Find food that excites you, or look for gaps in what is available. Discuss your ideas with your friends. Maybe even canvas. We will not rehash the strategies for developing a central food concept again here but return to the first chapter if you need some more inspiration.

When in doubt, start with your comfort foods or the foods you crave the most. Consider the restaurant makeup of your area. If there are plenty of sports bars, consider offering food that would match without competing. This puzzle of finding the right fit is important, so give it time. When you do come up with an idea, sit with it for a day to see how you feel about it. After all, whatever you choose, it will become a large part of your life for the immediate future.

Set Menu

Your menu will, in the mind of your customers, define your food truck. Even more than the name of your truck, your customers will connect with their favorite menu items, so ease-of-ordering definitely comes into play here. As you begin, it might be helpful to create a list of the foods you have been considering offering. They do not all need to include your primary food, but they should all fit into your overall concept or theme.

For example, a barbeque food truck might offer various sides, like grilled corn on the cob, that still fit with their concept and will not confuse customers or seem jarring. Of course, this is simply a general guideline. You might decide that the theme of your truck is Eclectic and choose to offer snacks from deep-fried pickles to ice cream sundaes. We are simply trying to communicate some basic guidelines to help you develop a cohesive menu; what you do with those guidelines is completely up to you. After all, we would absolutely stand in line for the Eclectic truck.

This is the point we are trying to make: Whatever it is, your menu must appeal to your customers. If this seems simple, it is because it is simple. Or perhaps not. You might love a particular food that few other people in your area do or personally prefer a level of spice that is off-putting to some customers. This does not mean scrapping your idea for spicy regional cuisine. It simply means catering your menu to your customers and offering options or variations that appeal to a wide range of tastes.

Crafting an appealing menu also means that you are not simply regurgitating or recycling existing menus. Recall the bagel truck example. You want to offer something unique, appealing, and affordable. At a minimum, your truck food should match two of these three descriptors to have any hope of profitability, and one of them must be to appeal, though we could perhaps substitute "incite curiosity" here as well. So, if you plan to serve more of a festival customer base, offering something new and intriguing matters slightly more than a specific food that will keep customers returning to your truck.

Each menu item you select must meet certain criteria to be a viable food truck food option. It must be able to go from the order to in the customer's hand within no more than six minutes, ideally half that time. This does not mean you must rule out food that requires longer to prepare, only that you might need to get creative with your advance prep strategies. At your truck, your customers are standing and waiting for their food, and the more customers you can serve, the more money you make by not losing those potential customers who are intimidated by the length of your line.

Keep the number of items you offer reasonable. This strategy can work to your advantage in different ways. You might offer one base item and multiple variations, such as a tossed salad that can be ordered with multiple different toppings. More common is to simply keep your offerings to between five and fifteen items, with at least one or two menu items operating as "sides" or extras. Another idea is to use overlapping food items to cut down on the total number of ingredients to purchase and prepare.

For each menu item that you consider, run it through a simple set of test questions to check that it meets your basic criteria for success. Does this item fit with my brand? Is this item unique, or is it offered by another food service location nearby? Can this item be prepared in my truck in less than ten minutes? And, ultimately, does this item appeal to my customers? You will be surprised how many options this eliminates.

If you are struggling to cut your total number of menu items down to less than fifteen, consider the quality of what you will be offering your customers. It is difficult in a food truck environment to maintain a high standard of quality if you are required to purchase and prepare hundreds of ingredients just to cover your menu. Remember your staff size and budget! We recommend keeping your menu even smaller. You can always add items after you have had your wheels under you for a few months. Start with 5 or 6 items for $5 or $6 each, for example.

Focus Testing

Develop a signature dish. This should be your most popular item and, as we discuss below, will get a place of prominence on your menu board. The easiest way to develop your signature dish is to actually cook and play around with different ways of preparing and serving your favorite menu items. Serve them to small groups of people and ask for their feedback. Ask for specific details. Which food is their favorite? Why? How is the sweetness or spiciness level? What would they add to the dish? What would they remove? Is it crispy enough? Does the paper bowl leak? Would it be easier to use a spoon than a fork? Would you prefer to eat this food with water or a soda? How is the saltiness? Asking thoughtful questions will give you valuable feedback. Trust us: people are always interested in being your guinea pigs for free or reduced-price food!

In fact, it is best to test out all your menu items this way to hone them into their best versions before your truck opens for business. If you have the opportunity, practice preparing your menu items inside the truck, too. Think of these practices as rehearsals for your big performance. In the days that lead up to opening day, it might be worth conducting a few full dress rehearsals with your staff. You should get their input as well. Being part of creating the menu for the food truck where you work can give your employees a sense of ownership. You might even have them vote on two different items to determine which one is on the menu.

While selecting and perfecting your dishes is important, it is equally important not to get too attached to specific dishes. We know you have worked hard to develop and perfect them, but if customers are simply not interested in or purchasing a certain menu item, take some time to consider why. You might work on adjusting the size of the dish or introducing some other changes to see if this makes the item more appealing. At a certain point, you may need to bid that item farewell. Think of your menu as a competition. Only the most competitive dishes get to stay on the board.

Serving

Your focus testing should include questions surrounding the serving of your products, too. If your food is dramatically too hot or cold, it might be unsafe for your customers, and you open yourself up to liability. Setting precise serving standards will help your staff maintain consistency in the products they serve, as well. Practicing or "rehearsing" your food truck service is a great opportunity to give your new staff some practice, too. Even things as simple as handing a plate or bowl down through a service window to a customer require practice. Naturally, you do not want to spill food all over your customers.

We suggest getting all your staff together and having each person cycle through the various roles they will be expected to perform, with one exception. Have them also fill the role of a customer to get a full sense of how your customers experience your food truck. As a bonus, your staff will get to taste all your menu items and be able to offer customers honest information in response to questions they might have.

Naming and Presentation

Your physical menu needs to be clear and easy to read and understand. This means the lettering should match your brand but be large enough to read from a reasonable distance, at least twenty feet away. Your customers are not expecting anything elaborate, just a few tasty options to choose from. If your branding is successful, they will already have an idea of what to expect as they approach your truck. It should not take them more than a minute or two spent looking at your menu to determine what they want to order. In fact, there are proven methods of presentation that can help you here, using psychological principles. Yes, we are really giving you the science of food trucks!

When listing prices, only use numbers and, if possible, round to a whole number or a price ending in 95 cents. The whole numbers let you cut down on space devoted to prices while using 95 cents rather than, say, 99 or 50 produces a psychological effect that focuses the brain on the dollar amount, giving the impression of a lower overall price. We know that this seems bizarre and illogical, but so is the human brain. Still, we recommend going with whole dollar amounts, ideally with the sales tax already baked in. Given the percentage of your customers who will pay cash, this will cut down on time spent making change.

But wait, there's more. Keeping dollar signs off the menu not only creates a cleaner look but also encourages people to spend more. It's that psychology again. Rather than different prices, offer two sizes for every menu item for two different prices. Why? Customers tend to opt for a larger size because it seems like a better deal, though the value to you will generally be higher for the larger size.

Perhaps the most important tip? Offer all your menu items for the exact same price. You might charge a little less for a side dish, but, in general, this is an excellent strategy for preventing your customers from comparing prices. It can also help simplify your signage. For example, you might offer all your menu items for $7.95.

All that saved space should be used for mouthwatering descriptions of each item. Give people a word picture. If these delectable descriptions are not something that you feel confident generating yourself, enlist outside help. Alternatively, you can check out how other food trucks and popular restaurants describe their meals. Consider what language appeals the most to your senses. You might even make a list of words and select from it the adjectives that best reinforce your brand. Once your customers picture your food, they will be even more eager to eat it.

Finally, it is all about location, location, location. The star of your menu show should be placed in the spot your customers will look to first. In English-speaking countries, this is the upper right-hand corner of your menu. For this reason, it makes sense to post your menu to the right of your service window from the customer's perspective. They should be able to look back and forth between your employees and that star menu spot easily, which will encourage rather than discourage conversation and make it easier for customers to reference the menu when ordering.

It seems counterintuitive, and many trucks keep their registers or POS systems to the left of the window, but the right side of the window makes the most strategic sense as the location for your register. While people tend to read left to right, they will be more willing to engage with your employees if this familiar pattern is flipped and they move through the ordering process right to left. Bear in mind that this is our 95 cents on the issue. It is your truck, and you can arrange it however you please.

We do advise purchasing a handheld card scanner, however, since some of your customers may have limited mobility or prefer not to hand you their credit card. If your customer window sits low enough, you can consider using a touchscreen that rotates, too. These screens allow you to include a tip prompt with various preset percentages. We still recommend a visible tip jar, however. Even if people are not paying with cash, the sight of the jar can serve as a gentle nudge. Just remember to empty your tip jar regularly and never leave your service window unattended.

Lastly, do not worry about including variations on your main menu board, even if you plan on allowing them. Food truck culture is reasonably casual and established, so people will generally feel comfortable asking you to leave something out of a dish if they would prefer. If that item is prepared in advance, you may need to tell them you cannot offer this. However, if you find you regularly receive requests for a specific variation, it may be worth incorporating it into your menu as a "customer favorite." Along the same lines, you might have the staff vote on their favorite menu item and note this in the description of that item.

Holiday and Seasonal Offerings

Though this will be a more important consideration later, after your food truck is on its feet (or wheels), begin considering how holidays will impact your business. In general, holidays are good business days for food trucks, regardless of the specifics of the holiday. Any government or school holiday will mean more potential customers on your street.

For now, consider the upcoming holidays and think about adding an additional special item to the menu leading up to or on the days of the holiday that relates to it in some way while remaining true to your food truck brand. Alternatively, you might add or alter the toppings on your dishes to match the holiday theme. If you prefer to keep your menu unchanged, you might simply purchase thematic paper goods. It is your truck, and, as such, these decisions are completely up to you.

Bear in mind, however, that certain types of food products will hold special appeal to your customers during the holidays and seasonally. For example, in the winter, people are far more likely to be drawn to a truck that offers hot chocolate or other hot beverages. Consider the climate when developing your seasonal menu. You might phase certain menu items in and out annually based on the time of year, for instance, swapping hot chocolate in the winter for cold smoothies in the summer. It is possible your food truck offerings will retain their appeal year-round, but most likely, you will need to consider seasonal adjustments and plan your source orders accordingly.

Value-Adding Promotions

Part of seasonal or holiday offerings might include short-term deals or promotions designed to capitalize on the temporarily increased number of potential customers. If you can use a simple two-for-one or similar deal to bring in more first-time customers during these high-traffic times, you may retain those customers later. However, you will need to estimate how offering such a deal will impact your sales and whether it is a viable option for your truck. The most successful promotions will play off of your truck's brand, serving a dual purpose as both a customer draw and additional advertising.

Budgeting

You will need to put in the time to consider how to budget for each season, holiday, or promotional change. For some trucks, it becomes worthwhile to hire additional temporary staff during busy holidays or seasons. If the daily operations of your food truck are demanding most of your time, consider hiring a back-of-house employee to keep track of and adjust for these changes sooner rather than later.

Chapter 10: Operational Considerations

Sourcing

One of the decisions you will need to make as a food truck business owner is how to source your ingredients and supplies. Sourcing simply refers to the companies or people from whom you purchase your wholesale ingredients and bulk quantities of supplies. These decisions will have an outsized impact on your monthly budget and the quality of the food you serve. As monthly expenses, food and supply costs will also factor into your decision on what to charge your customers and how many staff you can afford to hire.

Whether or not your city requires you to pay to use a commissary location, you will need to make certain you have some sort of staging area with the ability to store your ingredients at the appropriate temperatures overnight. You may use your existing restaurant to serve this purpose, or you might lease space from another business. When you are starting out, you may even convert a residential kitchen to serve the purpose. Of course, you will need to be aware of local regulations. Many areas restrict where food truck foods may be prepped.

Especially in your first few months, it will be challenging to accurately project your sales and purchase the correct quantities of ingredients. It may be worth running out of food a little early during your first month as you get a sense of how your demand will vary, rather than ending up with ingredients that are no longer fresh or usable. As you collect more data on your customer trends, you can adjust your orders to match demand. Of course, you will need to schedule yourself time to consider and place these orders from whichever sources you end up using.

Inventory awareness comes into play here as well. If orders are routinely filled late or inaccurately, it may be worth seeking out a new source. Your sourcing needs will depend primarily on your food truck offerings since many food sources are accessible globally. Generally speaking, this is because your food truck sources also supply restaurants, grocery stores, and other food service industry sellers. Bear in mind that you will generally need to identify your business by its registration number to shop from wholesale distributors and manufacturers without paying sales tax. It is wise to carry a hard copy of your business registration confirmation on you, such as folded inside your wallet, to use at local grocery stores if you realize you need to purchase extra of something to get you through the day, though you will still be paying a higher price than you would from a wholesaler source.

Once you know what you need and how much, you will be able to narrow down the best value sources for your truck. While you may come to rely primarily on a single source, it is wise to establish backup sources in the event that your supply chain is interrupted by weather or some other unforeseen circumstance. You will also need a verified address where the supplies can be delivered. Remember that any perishable items will need to be accounted for and stored immediately, and most food suppliers require a representative of the purchasing business to be present in person to receive the products they ordered. If you do not have a convenient delivery location, you may also have your food and supplies delivered to a local warehouse or distributor and pick them up there. In developing a system that works best for your truck, you should consider utilizing some combination of the following options:

Wholesalers

There are hundreds of wholesale distributors with directories available online. They offer food and beverage products in bulk to food service and grocery businesses. Based on your location, you may have access to a certain subset of these wholesalers, but there are also many who operate and ship internationally. Many food wholesale distributors base their offerings on a type of cuisine or culture. For example, Megafood International and CTC Food International offer European and Asian food products, respectively. The major distributors in the United States include Sysco, US Foods, United Natural Foods, and Performance Food Group. A simple internet search will reveal to you the many options you can choose from.

Local suppliers

Local and regional suppliers bring the added benefit of accessibility and speed. You may even work out a mutually beneficial arrangement on local products. These suppliers can include local grocers as well as small businesses based in your area. For example, there might be a nearby farm or meat processing plant that would allow you to set up smaller recurring orders on the condition that you drive out to pick up the products yourself.

Manufacturers

There are many, many options here. As with all your sourcing, quality drives price. Food manufacturers will often sell to vendors directly or connect you with the nearest product sales location. Though many operations are large, there are plenty of small companies and manufacturers where you can find uncommon products.

Co-ops

We will discuss food vendor membership organizations in a later chapter, but for now, consider how bundling your orders with other food trucks or local restaurants into bigger bulk orders can reduce the cost to everyone involved in the cooperative arrangement. Manufacturer and wholesaler discounts tend to increase with the number of orders, so identifying shared ingredient needs may end up saving you a lot of money. Look online to see if any existing co-ops might match some of your food purchasing needs. You may even consider starting your own co-op.

Local farmer's markets

If your truck emphasizes organic or healthy foods, sourcing from farmer's markets can be a great option and a marketable one. These foods cost slightly more than those from other sources, but your customers may also be willing to pay extra for this added value. For trucks offering exclusively plant-based foods, using only organic and locally sourced produce is a great way to reinforce your brand and commitment to your community. In such a situation, you are not only sourcing your ingredients but marketing in the process.

Shopping clubs

The odds are that you are familiar with Sam's Club, Costco, or BJ's already. These clubs pass on the savings of bulk shopping to consumers and, generally, the annual fees for membership are reasonably low. They offer the additional benefit of being easily accessible, and, as with any physical location, you are able to purchase items immediately without waiting for delivery. We recommend applying for membership to at least one local shopping club before beginning to purchase equipment for your truck since many smaller appliances will be available at a significant discount through these clubs.

Restaurant suppliers

These suppliers may cost more or require larger purchases than most food trucks support, but it is worth looking into restaurant supply stores and vendors as an option for sourcing dry goods or other shelf-stable items in bulk. You may need to work with a local restaurant that also orders from the supplier to have your deliveries bundled since it would not be cost-effective for a restaurant supplier to send a large truck to your location for only your relatively small orders. Timing is also an issue with any items that must be delivered.

It is also critical that you keep track of what is running low and will need to be ordered again well before you run out of any necessary supplies. You might have piles of ingredients ready to go, but without the paper serving dishes, you cannot sell your food. Digital shopping list applications can help you stay aware of what you will need. Instead of, or in addition to purchasing ingredients for cooking, you may also purchase pre-prepared foods from wholesale vendors. These foods may reach their sell-by dates soon after you receive them, so accurately judging how much to buy is vital to keeping your expense budget from overbalancing.

Of course, your local grocery stores and paper-goods stores are also great options in an emergency. You may also see whether local store managers are interested in setting up an arrangement to sell you certain items in bulk quantities. Here, it pays to have a business credit card set up and ready to use. Perhaps you run out of tomatoes and need to run to the store around the corner or send an employee with the company card. Make sure to require a receipt and to use your business ID number to save on sales tax.

Shop around and ask questions! The quality of your food begins with the quality of your ingredients and, by combining different sources, you should be able to source your food truck with the exact products you need to match your culinary vision. If you find that you are only moderately satisfied with an ingredient, it is smart to have other options readily available. While your orders are relatively small to wholesalers and restaurant suppliers, a local source is likely to notice that they have competition for your business and, as a result, may improve what they give you.

Security

Your entire business is based on the functioning of your food truck, so it makes sense to want to protect your investment. We dig into insurance in the following chapter, but there are many other practical steps you can take to avoid theft or damage to your truck. As a mobile vehicle, your truck is more vulnerable than a restaurant in the same ways that your car is more vulnerable than your house. For one thing, your house cannot be jacked up and towed away in the middle of the night, at least not easily. Developing precautionary habits from the outset can help you protect your business from some of the more common security issues.

As obvious as it may seem, locking your truck and taking your keys with you at the end of the day is a simple step that can make a big difference. It is easy to feel that the size of your food truck offers some protection, but it is still a vehicle with value and, as such, vulnerable to theft. If you do have a second key or set of keys made for your truck, keep them in a different, secure location and not inside your truck. Even if you are operating primarily out of your residence, you will likely have an office set up. It is smart to keep a fireproof lockbox in this secondary location with copies of your important documents. The documents themselves should be stored at a bank, though if this option is too expensive, your lockbox will work, too.

Unlike your personal vehicle, it is unwise to leave your registration in your food truck when you are not actively using it. You might consider keeping your registration with your keys or simply developing the habit of taking any registration documents with you when you lock up your truck each night. This will make your truck significantly less appealing to potential thieves, who will find it more difficult to sell your truck without these documents. Like your extra keys, keep these documents protected and secured until you need them, which should not happen often.

It is also smart to consider installing a security camera. Depending on your situation, you may choose to have this camera at the location where you park your truck or attached to the truck itself. Wherever you choose to place your surveillance camera, it should be visible in order to maximize its power as a deterrent. You should also install obvious signs calling attention to your security camera or alarm system. You may also decide to pay for an additional alarm system with these cameras. If you are required to park your food truck in a specific lot or commissary parking overnight, check that the location has active security cameras. Does this really matter to a potential thief or vandal? In fact, yes. Statistics support the use of security systems as a deterrent.

Picking a good parking location can be challenging if you work in a large city, though residential areas pose their own challenges. Try to find a location with good light in a secured garage or a high-traffic area. This includes food traffic. It may seem counterintuitive to leave your truck near people rather than tucked away out of sight, but statistics suggest this improves your odds of avoiding theft and vandalism. In some areas, the police may regularly patrol at night. If this is not the case, it is worth paying a security company to routinely check on your parked vehicle. Generally, commissary lots provide this service for a fee. Otherwise, you may be able to pool together with other food truck vendors who share the commissary lot to invest in a visible and active security system. After all the work you have put in, you do not want your business to vanish overnight.

If you do need to park your food truck on the street, a simple way to discourage theft is to turn your truck's front wheels at a sharp angle against the curb before setting your parking brake. Always set your parking brake! This arrangement makes it more difficult to easily tow your food truck. The same applies to the direction in which you park your truck in consecutive parking spaces. Backing into a parking space prevents a towing vehicle from easily accessing and lifting the rear of your chassis and locked rear wheels off the floor.

Again, this may seem like simple common sense, but remember to always have at least one person supervising your truck and to never leave the engine running or the keys in unless you are driving. As with any vehicle, it is a good idea to keep any valuables out of sight. With a food truck, you should never leave your POS system or any electronics inside except when you are operating your truck. This is another reason that a smaller, portable POS system can be a great asset to your truck. Unless it is a slow day, prepare yourself and your employees to eat their own meals at odd hours to accommodate rates of foot traffic.

It is also wise to think of your truck as you would a small restaurant. Apart from testing for quality, no food should be consumed in your kitchen. This is sometimes a personal choice and sometimes dictated by health codes, but we recommend distinguishing your "lunchtime" breaks from your workday by leaving the truck in your staff's capable hands to enjoy your own meal elsewhere. This can even help keep you more attentive when inside the truck and help reduce the risk of distraction and accidents.

An easy way to ensure all the listed basic security measures are met is to post a checklist that must be completed and initialed by whichever employee closes for the day, even if that person is generally you. But the best security measure might surprise you: a dog. Even the presence of a small dog near your stored vehicle is the best deterrent. Granted, you will not want a dog in your food truck, given food safety considerations, but if you do keep your vehicle parked at your home, it may be worth bringing home a puppy, too.

Knowing you have security measures in place can also give you some peace of mind, and, as a small business owner, you know exactly how hard that is to come by. In the end, you can only prepare as much as possible and face each obstacle as it comes. As you will see, insurance is one of the best ways to protect yourself against the unexpected. When traveling, too, purchasing extra insurance is worth the additional cost.

Food Preparation and Storage

The more able you are to set up your food preparation kitchen and truck kitchen arrangements to fit your needs, the less time you will need to waste getting your ingredients turned into complete meals you can sell. Carefully timing your deliveries ensures that they can be paid for and the purchased items safely stored is only the first piece of this elaborate juggling act that is running your small business. The same goes for the size of storage space your food truck supplies will require at appropriate temperatures. You will also need to determine the length of time required to prepare ingredients in your commissary space and schedule staff hours to complete this work and load your truck with the appropriate quantities before you leave for the day.

Our suggestion? Organize, organize, organize. Spreadsheets are your friends. Get a digital or physical calendar to keep track of all of your many daily, weekly, monthly, and annual obligations. Your employee shifts scheduling application with help with this, but you will need to schedule yourself time to work out the convoluted puzzle of who needs to be where, when. If you are not a naturally organized person, this will be all the more important. Consider bringing in a qualified assistant if you find that you are letting things slip through the planning cracks.

As much as we would like to set out step-by-step timelines and directions for efficiently preparing and cooking your food truck meals, we simply cannot. Your custom foods require custom preparation. If some of your meals are cooked to order, this equation is complicated by needing to calculate the amount of time it will take for your staff to prepare each meal before they can begin work on the next order. That said, this is the heart of your food truck business: the food. We are confident you will put in the time and energy ahead of time to help guarantee a quality result!

Cleaning and Maintenance Schedule

Part of your basic operational costs will include paying for cleaning products and regular truck maintenance. If you have no place to store larger quantities of supplies from your industrial suppliers, consider renting a simple space for this purpose. Over time, it is significantly less expensive to buy items like cleaning solutions in bulk and keep just enough on your truck that you do not lose valuable space. When handling industrial cleaners, be sure you and your staff are wearing protective gear and are careful to read all labels and warnings and not mix cleaners. Your food safety training should cover this, but it is worth reiterating.

Scheduling your truck's routine maintenance on low-volume days is a great way to maximize your productivity and keep the number of days your truck is open for business as high as possible. That said, be prepared for repairs to occasionally take longer than expected. It is smart to have a system of communication set up with your employees in the event of last-minute changes to the schedule. Many CMRs will include a messaging function, but it will likely be smart to have a phone call line, too. You should also be careful to include in the job description and employee handbook that such last-minute changes may occur. If you do not have your employees agree to this arrangement in some way, you may be responsible for paying them for those missed days.

There are many working parts involved in a running food truck, and each has the potential to cost you time and money and to support your customers' confidence in your business. For example, unique to your food truck is its generator. These devices are expensive, and repairs are costly. Keeping up with regular oil changes is a simple way you can prevent breakdowns. In fact, all of your equipment will last longer, even in the demanding conditions of a food truck, with proper maintenance.

As for the truck itself, the costs of routine maintenance are well worth it. Your garage will know best what to look for, but basic maintenance will involve oil changes, changing fuel filters, checking tire air pressure, tire rotation, checking battery connections, battery replacement, windshield repair, and wiper blade replacement. Most of these will need to occur every six to twelve months, depending on your mileage, road conditions, weather conditions, and overall climate.

You should also regularly check the windshield wiper fluid, transmission fluid, antifreeze liquid, brake fluid, and oil levels and inspect belts and hoses for early signs of damage. Many of these elements are relatively easy to check yourself. If you are unfamiliar with your food truck engine, ask someone knowledgeable to walk you through checking these important elements and schedule yourself time to perform these checks. You should continue to take your vehicle to a professional for regular maintenance, but performing some of these checks yourself will cut down on costs.

It is important to keep an emergency repair kit in your food truck. In addition to road safety and basic repair tools, it should contain enough emergency gear and supplies to support the maximum number of staff who work in your truck at a time. For example, your kit might contain an extra fire extinguisher, reflective triangles and road flares, jumper cables, a portable air compressor, a small toolbox, a stocked first aid kit, solar blankets, shelf-stable protein bars, and water bottles. While your safety inspection may involve keeping a first-aid kit in your truck, these extras are worth considering. Overprepared somehow never feels like too much in the event that something does go wrong. Prepare for the worst-case scenarios. Practice fire drills with your employees, for example. You might even have them use an older fire extinguisher in an empty parking lot so that they feel prepared to act in the event of a fire.

During the summer, you might increase your stock of bottled drinking water. During the winter, you should add an ice-scraper, road salt, and a de-icing fluid as well. If your region is subject to certain weather conditions, such as high volumes of snow, it is also worth investing in a set of snow tires you can use during the winter months. Some days you will need to make a judgment call regarding the weather conditions and the safety of your staff, and having appropriate tires reduces your risk of an accident.

Stay Organized

All told, your food truck business will require a startup cost anywhere between $30,000 and $120,000 if you purchase your truck, with monthly costs beginning at around $4,000 before labor, food, and supplies, which works out to a low-end figure of at least double that. If you are leasing or buying a food trailer, your final figures will skew slightly. Again, these monthly costs vary so dramatically that we would not want to give you a misleading estimate. Protecting your investment is important. As you make decisions about each aspect of your food truck, write them down, even if only as bullet points at first. This information will be consolidated and polished as part of your business plan.

Equally important is to put together a comprehensive spreadsheet for yourself to help you work out exactly how you will be able to meet your expense requirements. Be sure to include your initial costs for the truck, truck components, truck wrap, permits and licenses, a fire extinguisher, a website and branding consultant, POS system, shirts or other uniform gear, disposable serving supplies, basic cookware, any hiring expenses, and your initial inventory. Remember that will have some miscellaneous expenses or location-specific expenses in addition to these costs.

Your monthly costs will include your commissary location fee, internet and phone, truck fuel, truck insurance, business insurance, maintenance, repairs, supply restocking, food restocking, any ongoing marketing charges, and employee labor costs. Do not forget that if you opt for a lower overhead by renting your food truck, your monthly expenses will include that cost as well. Once you have some estimated numbers, you can work out the cost and number of meal orders you will need to complete each month to cover your expenses. And do not forget that cleaning calendar. We strongly advise adjusting to using a digital calendar application if you have not already. This will allow you to track tasks and events grouped by type and, as your business expands, be valuable information that can easily be shared among your staff.

Chapter 11: Establishing a Community Presence

Know Your Neighborhood

Being active in your community offers your food truck multiple benefits and opportunities to grow. Not only will you strengthen customer relationships and promote your brand, but if you eventually decide to pursue a brick-and-mortar location, add trucks, or expand in any way, community support will improve your ability to effectively run a crowdfunding campaign or simply spread the word as a free and effective marketing tool.

Word-of-mouth, physical and digital, will be the best promotion of your brand. With your local community passing on their enjoyment of your food truck, you will have more opportunities for special events and even expanding your operation to include multiple trucks or a physical location. There are as many ways to connect with your community as there are food trucks, but we have found several specific strategies from which food trucks can benefit. This chapter investigates these methods of engagement to help get you thinking about strategic ways to approach your community right from the beginning.

The people who live in your city or town do so for a reason. The odds are that they feel a connection with their city, and your business can join them in that shared bond of community pride. Though it is possible to work out endorsements with local celebrities, businesses, or the city government itself, even something as simple as creative menu names or local sport team specials can actively engage the community. You know best what resonates with your community. You might live in a heavily arts-influenced area and could commission or work with a local artist to develop a special logo or branded merchandise, such as screen-printed shirts. Regional festivals or local anniversaries specific to your city might also provide opportunities to share in community celebrations.

While planning specific activities or events that involve your community can wait until your truck is up and running, it is important to begin setting up your truck culture in a way that sets a solid foundation for these later efforts. As you serve food from your truck, remember to engage with your customers and encourage your staff to do the same. Simple conversations can give you access to all sorts of local information. You may discover exciting events, recurring or specific, and find out which businesses that are active in your area are customer favorites. Perhaps a local non-profit organization is planning a weekend of cleaning or gardening in a community park. Consider approaching the organizers to see if you could donate meals or even just free beverages to the volunteers.

Similarly, try to find out if any local charity events could benefit from reduced-price catering. The presence of your truck and brand will not go unnoticed as you help support positive growth and development within your community. This strategy will be specific to your area of operation, of course. If your truck is oriented more toward festivals and events for which you must regularly travel and are rarely physically in the same location, there are still important aspects of customer engagement to consider.

Each event has its own culture, and most of its participants will share or understand a certain set of values as part of their participation. This sounds more complex than it is. In fact, what we mean is simply this: research and pay attention to the culture of whatever event you will be attending in advance. This way, you will be able to connect with and relate to your customers at the event. Consider, for instance, renaming your menu options to fit a relevant music genre or finding out if you can outfit your staff with festival shirts. Be creative. As much as people will approach your truck because they want something to eat, what they are likely to remember is how they were treated. When you engage with event culture, you are communicating to your customers that you respect their values and are supporting them in enjoying this experience they wanted to be a part of enough to pay to attend.

This advice applies to trucks that only occasionally serve at festivals and events, too. However, if your truck does have a "home base" community, remember to respect it and not betray your customer's understanding of your brand by altering your core principles for the sake of some extra sales at an event. To give a practical example, if your dessert truck is known to be child-friendly, you should consider how to approach a heavy-metal rock festival and, perhaps, whether it matches your brand to attend at all. You will need to weigh the impact of these choices against the loyalty of your primary customer base and come up with the best solution for you.

Your most potent tool in connecting with your community is also your most effective marketing tool: social media. Plan a social media strategy that includes local stores or history and helps promote other local businesses or trucks. Your truck might even join crowdfunding or similar campaigns to support growing businesses or non-profit efforts. Moreover, all your community-based activities can be tracked on your social media feeds, letting your customers see how committed you are to becoming a contributing part of your shared community.

Remember not to forget the bottom line while enjoying participating in local events. Alert your social media manager of the relevant information so that they can get quality photos and quotes from attendees to use to promote your business online. If you do not already have a dedicated social media or marketing manager, assign one of your staff to take responsibility for documenting your presence at an event. They would also be able to promote the event beforehand on your various feeds. The ideal person for this task might be your office or "back-of-house" staff person since they will not be preoccupied with food service. Or it might be worth asking or paying a friend or professional to attend and take plenty of pictures.

As you become more established, or if there is not as active a local community in your area, you might choose to commit your brand to a specific cause to begin building associations in the minds of your customers between your brand and some positive activism. Do not underestimate the power of a food truck to inspire your customers into charitable participation. Consider which causes you personally support or want to support and think of ways you can leverage your small business to support that cause. You might offer discounts for charitable donations or simply use your truck to promote a specific shelter or cause. We recommend avoiding introducing anything that might be off-putting to your customers, however, so it is best to steer well clear of politics!

As an active food truck, you may find you are unable to spare the extra days that some of these community engagement suggestions might require. If this is the case, don't worry! There are always other options to build brand awareness. Even monetary donations or donations of products, gift cards, or merchandise to local fundraisers will help cement your community presence and raise your brand awareness. You can even use your online platforms to promote these events. The more often people are reminded of your truck with positive associations, the better.

Working with local businesses, events coordinators, and news organizations to arrange for advertising is another good method for bringing your brand to the forefront of people's minds. We will discuss the festival circuit in more depth in a later chapter, but consider that even local events like fairs, charity runs, concerts, sporting events, and even farmer's markets provide great opportunities to engage with your community. However, when working with smaller events, do not forget that you may need to submit applications early as corporate sponsorship and participation openings may fill up quickly. Many of these options require only a small commitment of your time that is well worth the free advertising that comes with it.

That said, when you first open, you will have a lot on your plate. Do not feel pressured to get out there on your first day. You will need to devote most of your energy to getting your physical truck off to a solid start, and we simply want to make you aware of this important element of your future success so that you can identify potential engagement opportunities right from the beginning.

Again, you will know best how to engage with your community. An area with lots of young families might be a great opportunity to sponsor a youth soccer club or similar youth organization. This is more of a financial commitment, so do not feel pressured to seek out this level of engagement right away, but do keep in mind that the more you give to your community, the more they will want to give back to you.

Do not forget to be creative! Remember that your truck is a part of the community in its own right, simply by existing as part of the food culture of your area. Think of ways to acknowledge this and celebrate your business. You might throw your truck a birthday party similar to a block party or pair up with a dessert truck to offer a "full meal" discount. Your truck's success is built on your hard work, but even that means little if you are unable to engage with your customers. In larger cities, your strategy for engaging with your community will look very different from in a small town, of course, but there are always ways to connect with people. If you are anything like many food truck business owners, this will prove to be the part of your job that you will enjoy the most.

Branded Products

Offering branded products tends to be most successful after your brand is reasonably established and you are looking to grow. An exception to this is to use these products as part of crowdfunding campaigns or pitches to give donors a physical connection to your brand. You will have to decide your approach to and budget for marketing and merchandise. Whenever you decide that your truck can afford to increase its marketing budget, branded products are a great way to reward customer loyalty. They can include everything from mugs to umbrellas to miniature toy food trucks.

The only real limitation, other than cost, is that your choice of products should in some way reflect your brand, and their design should fit that brand, too. If your truck sells cupcakes, for instance, you might offer custom cupcake tins and custom baking mix. These products also offer more opportunities to partner with other local businesses that might be interested in selling your branded items. Though products serve a marketing purpose, it is important to ensure they are not netting negatively financially. That is, the cost of creating your products should not be greater than the amount made through their sale. Since you will need a certain amount of startup inventory, you will need to consider, in a similar way to your ingredient order, how much inventory to begin with. The benefit of branded products is that you can usually start with a small quantity to get a sense of how quickly the items will sell and, from there, reevaluate the cost to the customer that you will be charging.

As a final note, be aware of the differences in sales tax in some places between food and non-food items. In the United States, different states require different tax percentages and different sets of items that are offered tax-free, though some of these regulations are established at the federal level. Your POS (Point Of Sale) software will be programmable to account for these differences. Still, you will need to set the amount that your customer will be charged or at the very least confirm that the appropriate sales tax is being applied to the different products based on your location or locations. This may simply mean confirming that the system's GPS is accurately reading your food truck's current location, but, as with all things involving money, it is worth double-checking.

You will also need to decide how to source your branded products. Do you want to work with a small local screen-printing shop? Some important considerations will include whether the business can support the quantity and quality you need at an appropriate cost to you. So, will you set up recurring orders or order as needed? What do you want the quality of your branded products to be? Do you want to pay for a professional design or go with a simple logo? We did warn you that a food truck owner's whole job is, essentially, to continuously make decisions.

Copyright and Trademark

We will not delve in-depth into intellectual property law here since this is covered in another chapter, but it is important to consider prioritizing pursuing a brand trademark when selling branded products. The likelihood of someone selling unauthorized imitations of a design you use on a tee-shirt, or imitating your signature recipes is significantly higher as your brand's presence and popularity increases. Your logo and food truck name are unifying aspects of your food truck brand, so protecting them is key.

As you are selecting a name for your truck, performing a basic trademark search enables you to avoid choosing a name that has already been registered. For a fee, you can also register your own food truck to avoid any conflicts later, though how you choose to enforce your trademark is largely your choice. Similarly, copyrighting your logo is a simple way to protect it. If you use a marketing or branding company, they may offer an option to assist with the legal side of this, though registration is reasonably straightforward. Once you have this layer of protection, it will be easier to be confident that your branded products will hold their appeal. For details on this process, which can be quite tedious and lengthy, consult the chapter addressing legal issues.

Rebranding

If you cannot at first afford to fully develop a brand concept or are leasing a food truck until you can purchase your own, you might consider opening without a fully realized brand with a planned later rebranding once you have accumulated sufficient funds. Essentially, a rebrand allows you to reinvigorate or fully realize your brand, polishing existing materials or generating new ones to reshape your brand image. One of the significant benefits of holding off on your branding is that it allows you time and practice to feel out exactly what you want your brand to be and how you want to present your truck to your customers. This allows to iron out some of the new-business kinks before committing to a definite direction or unified brand, so it is definitely something to consider if you are still uncertain of some of the more central elements that will be important to your food truck's brand, such as cuisine, name and logo, and culture.

Sometimes, this process becomes necessary if your existing brand is exposed to some form of extreme negative publicity, but more often, it is used to allow for a sort of soft open to your food truck. That said, it is generally best to prepare for the worst. Have an action plan in place in the event that your truck does in some way experience a bout of negative publicity. This could be anything from customers getting seriously ill to a viral video of an employee insulting a customer. The best way to avoid the potential for the kind of negative press that demands a complete rebrand is to ensure your staff all receive and internalize the appropriate training in everything from food safety practices to appropriate professional conduct. Even then, mistakes will happen. Having a media strategy in place allows you to respond to such incidents immediately and effectively. If you hire a social media or marketing manager, this will be the ideal person to help you develop such a strategy.

However you go about it, it is wise to consult a professional at some point. What may intuitively seem to be the appropriate response to a situation may only make matters worse for the people involved and for your food truck brand. There is a reason they are paid to address these issues, and it is because they have the expertise and the experience to do so in a way that minimizes fallout for your business. They can help you plan a recovery strategy or recommend another approach you might not have even considered.

That said, management training often involves receiving training in handling sensitive issues that could or already have resulted in negative publicity or customer interactions. It is important to remember that if you are going to be the face of your brand, you should approach your own education as an effective tool that helps you build a successful business. Do not neglect your own training. Consider enrolling in a free online management course through YouTube or audit a class through a local college. Not only will you be advancing your own education and increasing your set of skills and knowledge, but your business will also benefit directly, and you will feel more confident to take decisive action as a strong leader of your food truck team.

Whatever its purpose, once you have built enough to afford a rebrand, it is worth committing to a new website and social media upgrades, as well as the more fully developed branding mechanisms discussed in previous chapters. Why is this? In today's world, it will be difficult to maintain a successful business without an online presence because so much of how people seek out and share information related to restaurants and foods happens in digital spaces and forums. When you choose not to participate in social media platforms, you are choosing not to engage with a significant number of potential customers and limiting the potential growth of your food truck.

Chapter 12: The Circuit

In the previous chapter, we covered how your food truck can make the most of local community involvement. In this chapter, we will investigate what is known as the festival circuit. This simply refers to the series of recurring annual festivals and similar-style events that rely primarily on mobile food vendors to feed the participants. Serving food at these events is one of your options for increasing your average revenue each day, particularly during the summer season. Of course, getting involved in festival vending comes with its own set of requirements. You must successfully apply, carefully plan your strategy and ordering, travel to and from the venue, and maintain a grueling pace, but, if you can manage it, the festival circuit or a limited selection from it can be quite lucrative for a food truck business.

The first, and perhaps the most important, decision you will need to make regarding festivals is which events match your food truck brand. For example, a salad truck might not have much success at certain concerts or Renaissance festivals. You will need to do your research to determine the types of food trucks that tend to be most successful at different events. Depending on your location, you will likely get to choose between many events to determine which are the best fit for your truck. Strategically planning to attend specific events can give your food truck a financial boost, but remember that even festivals are no guarantee. As always, weather can result in canceled events or dramatically limited attendance.

Festivals also involve a significant investment. You will need to pay application and parking fees as well as gas and other travel expenses. In theory, driving from Point A to Point B is not a huge undertaking. In reality, you will need to factor in preparing your truck for travel and even where to stop for meals on the trip, since your truck is not as easy to simply take through a fast-food drive-thru as most personal vehicles and security overnight might be an issue. Food trucks are also not set up to be particularly comfortable to travel in for an extended period of time.

In addition to this, many event organizers charge a percentage of your revenue, which might force you to dramatically raise your prices to cover your costs. If this is something that goes against your vision for your brand and your customer relationships, festivals might not be for you. But festivals are not obligatory when you are running a food truck. There are plenty of ways to operate a profitable truck without participating in large festivals at all. You will need to decide whether serving at festivals offers an overall value to your business and, if so, which festivals to attend and how to mitigate your financial risk because festival participation does involve an upfront financial investment.

If you do decide to participate in festivals, you need to be confident that your investment will still result in a profit. This will likely involve limiting your menu offerings during the festival to ensure a quick turnaround for orders and hiring temporary staff to help handle the volume. It is also a good idea to consider rewarding their hard work financially because festival work is fast-paced and non-stop. You may even rearrange your standard cooking arrangements so that you are only assembling rather than doing the cooking during a festival since you will not have access to your usual commissary.

Once you have determined which festivals match your brand and complete the budgeting to determine whether attendance at these events is likely to result in a net profit worth the extra time and effort, you will need to make a detailed plan of everything, starting with when to put together and send your initial application to participate in an event.

Festival Planning

Applications

One of your first challenges is getting accepted by the organizers of your chosen event. As a new truck, you might have less success at first. Essentially, you need to be able to convince organizers that your truck will bring value to their event. This is a different sales approach than the one you will have already taken when pursuing business financing or when marketing yourself to customers. Your business is, by now, established, and you understand what it has to offer. You need to match that offering with the needs of the event organizers.

Larger events are highly competitive, so do not be discouraged if it takes several applications before you are accepted to a festival. To better your odds, spend enough time on your application to ensure you are marketing yourself well. This is no time to be modest. The best applications get right to the point and give organizers a precise and favorable picture of your food truck. Be descriptive and pack a punch, but do not overdo it on length. Keep your appeal brief and to the point. Include whatever figures are requested, but also link to your online sites and any positive press your truck has received. To demonstrate your commitment, you can also include the menu you would offer with appetizing pictures. Bullet points are a good idea, too. A special menu selection that matches the demands of the event is a great way to demonstrate that you have thought through your attendance and are already committed to making you, the venue, and the event team successful by offering an appealing product that meets the demands of festival attendees.

Remember that organizers are on a timeline and likely have to process hundreds of applications. They want you to give them the key facts, and you need your application to stand out. Reference how your customer base overlaps with the festival participants and, if they support your argument for inclusion in the festival, cite your financial figures as evidence of your truck's popularity.

Permits

Though you are fully licensed to operate in your usual business area, you will need to carefully check and confirm that you have all the necessary permits to serve food at the festival venue, even if it is in the same state or city where you usually operate. For instance, if you are removed from your commissary, you will need to obtain a permit to temporarily use a facility near the festival. Generally, the organizers will be able to give you all the information you will need since their event permits involve planning for a set number of food vendors. There are often already arrangements in place for a commissary kitchen or the equivalent that can be or is sometimes required to be, used by the participating food trucks and other mobile vendors.

You should also check your insurance policy. You and your employees may be covered already, or you may need to add additional short-term liability coverage. It is smart to check that your commercial automobile insurance is up to date, too. Your chances of a breakdown increase the longer you are required to be on the road traveling. You may opt to pay for a roadside assistance service for the period during which you are traveling or have a "rescue team" on-call or a plan prepared in the event of some mechanical or other issues that involve more than simply replacing a tire.

Annual Calendar

Festivals are, generally, outdoor events, which means that they are also seasonal. While there are winter or off-season events that hire food trucks, the biggest opportunity is in the summer months. Of course, you will need to begin planning for attendance well in advance of the season, even as early as a year before in the case of some hugely popular and well-attended annual events, like Coachella.

The summer season is ideal for capitalizing on outdoor festivals, but you should balance your availability to your community customer base with your festival commitments. Here, your social media connections will be a valuable resource. Ideally, your customers will be able to track your truck's location through tracking applications, so if you have not already set this up, definitely consider doing so before the event. You should also generate buzz through your online connections leading up to the event, letting your customers and potential customers know that you will be attending.

You should also consider how draining festival work can be. Protect you and your staff by scheduling plenty of recovery time between events if you plan to return to your usual area of operation and maintain a presence there rather than traveling directly between events. No matter how you plan to schedule your time, creating a calendar and keeping records is crucial to your future success. If an event turns out to be poorly organized or has low attendance, or if for whatever reason your truck is less successful, you should reconsider participating in future years and making notes of these reasons can also enable you to offer this valuable information to other food truck owners within your network in exchange for their insights.

While we have referred to these events with the inclusive term "festival," they can range from single-day concerts to trade shows and vehicle events to conferences that, rather than resulting in immediate profits, are expenses with longer-term benefits. The NFTA, National Food Truck Association, lists various resources and links to confirmed events. Food industry events and trade shows offer you and your team the chance to network and are often specific to the types of food you offer. When planning to attend a trade show, you should consider that the cost of attendance is an investment in the benefits that will result. These events give you a sense of new developments within your industry and can inspire you to try new approaches in your own business. Specifically, there are so many new technologies impacting the digital marketing landscape that it can be useful to see examples of how your fellow food truck businesses have utilized various applications and which seem to produce the best results. Obviously, these events do not net the profits of festival events where your truck will be providing food service, though there may be avenues for offering food service in some capacity.

Though the complete list of festivals is different every year, some of those best known for their food truck offerings in the United States include The World's Largest Food Truck Rally in Florida, L.A. Street Food Fest in California, Sea Isle City Food Truck Fest in New Jersey, Chicago Food Truck Festival in Illinois, Columbus Food Truck Festival in Ohio, Atlanta Street Food Festival in Georgia, Seattle Street Food Festival in Washington, Main Street Food Truck Festival in Arkansas, H&8th Night Market in Oklahoma, Street Eats Food Truck Festival in Arizona, Eat The Street in Hawaii, Taste of Three Cities in Pennsylvania, and Cape Cod Food Truck And Craft Beer Festival in Massachusetts.

Though it is completely unrealistic to think you might be able to attend all these events (for one thing, some of the dates overlap), you should absolutely think about trying to attend the event nearest you. Not only is the experience surreal—after all, these festivals boast thousands of trucks—but you will have the chance to get great ideas to apply to your own food truck, in standard operation, or in festivals specifically. If you plan to operate your food truck as a seasonal business, you should plan your travel between events as strategically as possible. This will mean having not only a plan but backup plans for each event. While the larger food truck festivals likely will not shut down for something like adverse weather conditions, there is always the possibility that something might disrupt even the best-laid plans. So, as they say, plan accordingly.

Travel Costs and Considerations

Your travel expenses will depend on your situation, including how far you will need to travel. You may need to bring along another vehicle to transport your staff, inventory, supplies, and whatever luggage they will need for the length of the festival. Or you may be able to tow a trailer behind your truck. At the beginning of the festival season, it is wise to take your food truck to your garage for a tune-up and repairs, too.

Successful business operation all comes down to planning, planning, planning. This is the key to festival success. It is wise to make lists of the additional inventory and supplies you will need to bring with you, including back-ups, and plan your orders in advance. We recommend going so far as to mark down the dates on which you will need to place each order. You also do not want to run out of things early in a festival environment when you cannot simply return to your usual commissary every night. When competing directly with other food vendors at larger events, make certain your truck and staff are operating at and looking their best. This involves planning, too. It can even come down to bringing along a tire brush to clean your wheels and other truck cleaning gear. Arrive early and, as any experienced festival vendor will tell you, load up on coffee.

In general, at festivals, it is customer service that is noticed, remembered, and reviewed online more than any other aspect of your food truck, including the food itself. So, while a festival can be great exposure for your food truck brand, it can be potentially disastrous, too. While food truck-specific festivals are a great opportunity to market and network, your truck will also be compared directly with other competing food trucks, and, as much as these festivals are designed as a celebration of food, it is actually the experience of your truck that festival attendees will latch onto. This makes sense since anything that distinguishes you from the competition is going to stand out. While this could be a great opportunity to generate hype for your truck, do not simply assume that because your truck is present at a food truck festival that people will view it positively. While you may still generate a significant profit during the festival, negative reviews after the fact will cause lasting damage to your reputation and brand.

We cannot overemphasize enough the importance of making your truck more than the food you serve. While festivals are usually a race to serve as many customers as you conceivably can as quickly as possible, this pace can have a dramatic impact on tempers and energy and, as a result, your customer's experience of your truck. Someone might get their meal in two minutes flat, but even delicious food is not enough to make up for a brusque interaction with an employee or embarrassment when their credit card chip is being uncooperative, and the harried staff is unable to hide their annoyance. Why is this? There is proven psychology behind this phenomenon, which essentially shows that emotional responses produce more vivid and lasting memories than sensory experiences. Preparing your staff for what to expect, as much as possible, is the best way to set your food truck up for success. Practice your festival-specific menu and consider timing your orders to work out where you can introduce more efficient processes. During the festival itself, you can also take notes on anything that might improve your festival participation in the future.

As an additional consideration, there may be certain restrictions on staffing hours that originate with the venue or even the state or city. Check that you have adequate staff to cover the demands of not only your planned hours but the legal requirements in place. If the area has set a higher minimum wage rate, you may also need to adjust your compensation to match.

Your Truck Network

Some of your most valuable resources regarding festival participation will be other experienced food truck owners. There are many membership organizations and online resources for food truck business owners that can provide you with an idea of what to expect to plan effectively. The website of the NFTA, National Food Truck Association, provides a wealth of information regarding the specifics of festival permits and relevant links to more informative sites. Joining any national and regional food truck organization gives members great access to time and cost-saving methods and resources at every level of truck operation.

That said, your community connections are a great resource, as well. There is nothing quite like some first-hand experience, and we advise learning all you can from the people who have been in your position. Finding a truck owner who serves food similar to yours will be the most helpful because they will have the best insider tips for how to prepare your specific food truck for work at festivals.

As a final note here, festivals are also a great way to get to know and be exposed to many other food truck owners and employees. You can learn a lot simply by keeping your eyes open, but it is a great idea to take any available opportunities to network. You do not work out of a traditional office, and it can be difficult to connect with other food trucks that do not operate in your immediate area, particularly if they do not maintain an active online presence. Get to know these people who work in the industry you all share. Not only can you find community, but exchanging information can benefit everyone, and seasoned festival food truck owners will have all sorts of valuable insights and tips to offer. Remember that you may not have time for an hour-long discussion, but even a simple exchange of contact information can yield all sorts of benefits later.

Take business cards with you and consider including your personal contact information on some of them. If you do not have current business cards printed, get them. As a small business owner, you should always have these cards on you. In fact, it is smart to develop a habit of always looking for opportunities to promote your truck or connect with people who might, even in an indirect way, provide some benefit to you or your business. If nothing else, it does not hurt to spread awareness of your brand as much as possible.

Chapter 13: Selling Your Truck

Decisions, Decisions

Deciding to sell the food truck you worked so hard to grow into a flourishing business is not a decision we expect you to make lightly. If you are just starting your business, it is highly unlikely that you will need to consider selling your truck for a while, but with starting any small business, it is crucial to remain aware of your options and the overall value of your business and assets.

Obviously, many factors may play into this choice to sell. You may be trying to relocate or want to pivot into another industry. You may simply have grown your business as far as possible within your local community and be looking to branch out into a bigger city or to start another truck. Perhaps you are even interested in starting a brick-and-mortar restaurant or have only ever planned to operate a food truck for a year or two.
One common reason for selling a food truck is that your business is still growing, but you as an owner are unable or uninterested in managing more people. Maybe your custom food concept turned out to be less successful than you anticipated in your area, and you are ready to cut your losses. Though we hope this last is not the case, we understand that owning a small business is challenging and a huge commitment. Sometimes, the smartest option is to sell.

Whatever your reasons, selling a small business can be incredibly stressful, and there are some basic steps you can take to make the process easier. Before you act, be certain you have considered the decision from every angle. Talk to people you trust and have them help you weigh the pros and cons. It is easy to get caught up in our own perspective and forget that we bring our bias to the table, particularly when feeling the weight and pressure of a big decision where a lot of money is involved. Do not rush. Unless you are on a deadline, it is best to sit with any major decision for at least a few days.

Remember, you have more options than just staying in your current role within your business or selling. Your desire for a change might not necessitate selling your business. If there are financial concerns, it might be worth modifying your approach, working out staffing issues, or rebranding. If you feel you are stagnating or ready for something else personally, you might even consider bringing in someone to fill your active role or promoting a manager to maintain daily operations. If you think you will ever want to use your unique brand again for another venture or food truck, consider holding onto your business and selling only your physical assets, like your truck and appliances. Whatever your reasons or approach, if you are ready to move on to the next chapter in your business career, be prepared to do some work to get your business ready for sale.

Once you are certain, it is time to do some work before you can set a price and find a buyer. As with any business, you want to make certain you are appropriately valuing your food truck business as a whole. Your brand itself has value, and you may simply be selling your physical truck to someone rather than your business and brand. It is vital not to undervalue the work you have committed to growing your customer base and brand loyalty. Intangible aspects of your business can seem difficult to value, but one simple way of putting your efforts into perspective is to look at your first year and compare it to your current earnings. In a concrete way, this difference reflects some of that work.

That said, you may not have owned your business long enough to see as much of a profit impact yet. That is okay! You know your business best, but you might be too close to it to have a complete picture of its worth. Assembling a business portfolio will help you create a comprehensive picture of your business for the purposes of explaining and valuing it. As with your original executive summary for pursuing financing, a business portfolio will include all the relevant information about your business. Instead of projections, of course, you will now have actual sales data and financial statements. There are some basic steps you can follow to put together a complete portfolio that will communicate a true sense of your food truck business and equip you to get the most out of your sale.

Formalizing Your Business Portfolio

The first tangible thing you can do to prepare for sale is to organize your financial statements. Practically speaking, this means documenting every aspect of your business finances for the past three years or for however long you have been operating if you started your business within the past three years. Good record keeping from the outset will make this process much easier. You will need to pull together profit and loss statements, revenue balance sheets, and complete tax records. You should also list all your physical assets: your truck, appliances, and equipment, and make copies of any ongoing financing or leasing statements. You can estimate the value of these parts of your business by researching comparable items up for sale through online resale sites or factoring in depreciation from the original price. Remember that the brand, condition, age, and maintenance records all factor into the current market value. Your current inventory of product and supplies are also an important list to include.

Essentially, any part of your business with value should be clearly documented. It is important that you not make guesses as to the value of any of your assets, however. If you are uncertain, consult a professional within the industry. You can get a signed statement of value for any piece of equipment.

Though some of this will not be transferable, you should also prepare documentation of your different forms of insurance, your permits, licensing, detailed employee agreements and wage statements, and any ongoing sourcing contracts. Your POS system will be able to generate reports similar to those used for tax purposes. Business banking statements will show the business's current profitability and provide a buyer with a realistic picture of what your business can accomplish for them. Finally, you will also need to provide detailed recipe information since your food is a critical piece of your business. It might be difficult to give up your trade secrets, but do not forget your commitment to your customers. This information also increases the value of your business to a potential buyer.

Appraisal

As you put together a business portfolio of your assets and liabilities, you will be able to provide a professional with concrete numbers that demonstrate your food truck business's profitability. Why, you might ask, if you have the complete picture of your business financially, should you bring in a professional? To get a realistic market value estimate, it is well worth paying for an independent financial analysis. This is not an area where you can afford to make a mistake. Overvaluing your business might waste time you do not have, and undervaluing it can result in unnecessary financial loss to you.

When looking for a professional to consult about getting an estimate, be aware that the food truck industry is still in its early years. You may need to hire a professional with more practical experience in restaurant evaluation, for example, a well-established industry. You can be confident that these professionals will still have a good sense of what to look for when valuing your food truck business. You may also request that your bank consult whatever professional they trust to make an independent analysis.

Your insurance and premiums will provide any financial professional with a reasonable place to begin when valuing your business since insurers do much of the same work to determine the worth of your business assets as an actual cash value (ACV), a term that refers to the direct monetary value of the components based on the original cost of your truck and equipment added to the cost of the labor necessary to install that equipment. This approach is also referred to as finding the current value (CV), as opposed to the replacement cost (RC), which is the approach often taken with businesses operating out of physically set locations and buildings.

The food truck evaluation will also consider what is known as the personal property of your business, the items contained within your truck that are not actually installed in any way, simply stored there. This would include everything from supplies to cookware, even fire extinguishers, and extra fuel. This process will be dramatically simplified if you purchased some or all of your equipment brand new and have not owned them long since the sales price will still be an accurate measure of value. With a used truck and equipment, you will need to factor in improvements you have made, anything from replacing engine parts to upgrading countertops.

We mentioned your business personal property, anything not attached; you will also need to assess the attached equipment. This includes literally anything that has been installed permanently, from plumbing, electric, and gas lines to bolted-down cooking equipment. The same rules of thumb apply for evaluating price with new and used attached equipment, except that you should be sure to add the cost of labor for installing each item. This does not mean only the cost you paid someone to install your oven. It refers to any installation work, even the hours you spent doing your own installation of equipment. This makes it even more necessary to document your own labor as you set up your food truck business. Not only does it give you a better picture of where your hourly rate sits, but it will also make the process of valuing your business much simpler in the future.

Depreciation sounds intimidating, but it is actually quite simple to apply to your equipment. The current wisdom is that commercial kitchen equipment (and, in fact, personal kitchen equipment as well) has a life of approximately 20 years. Based on this assumption, you first determine the cost of each item bought. You also determine how much of the life of each item has elapsed so far as a percentage of 20 years. For example, if your brand and model of refrigerator costs $2000 to purchase brand new and it is 12 years old, you will determine that it has lived 60% of its estimated lifespan. This equation is performed by dividing the current age by the total 20 years and multiplies that fraction by 100. Taking 60% of the original cost of $2000 leaves you with $1200. If you had the refrigerator installed for $100, you would add that cost as well, giving you $1300 as the current value.

But be sure you do not forget any other alterations that might have introduced additional value. Perhaps you purchased additional shelves or painted the equipment to match your truck. These are known as aftermarket alterations, and their cost should be added to your total as well. There are resources you have access to online through food truck builders websites that can help you if you get stuck, such as the list provided by InsureMyFood.com.

You will use the same formula to determine the value of non-attached equipment, based on a similar approximate 20-year total for each piece of gear or equipment. This includes your small appliances, POS devices, and, importantly, anything not bolted into your truck. The example above of the refrigerator would need to be reclassified within this category if it were not bolted into your truck. As you perform these calculations, keep records of how you are determining the value of each item. This is an easy way to demonstrate the accuracy of your total once you add all these amounts together. You may be pleasantly surprised by exactly how much your food truck is worth since you will have acquired some of these items over time and contributed to their value as a side-effect of altering or improving them to match your food truck's needs.

Calculating the depreciation of your truck works in precisely the same way, except that the industry standard for most food truck vehicles, those weighing approximately 12,000 pounds, is a 5-year lifecycle. Check this against other vehicles and consult experienced food truck owners or sellers, however, because this time frame can shift over time up to around seven years. Also, be careful not to add any aftermarket upgrades to more than one category. For example, if you account for a mechanical outlet replacement as part of the value of your truck, you cannot also apply it to the attached equipment generator that connects to it.

All of this probably seems like a lot of information to take in. However, the process itself is straightforward. The trickiest aspect of determining value will be making certain to account for every single item and every possible improvement. Here, your recordkeeping is what will help or hurt you the most. If you have documented every repair and installation, you will have a much better chance of arriving at an estimated value that accurately reflects the true value of your food truck.

Brokers and Buyers

While the choice of whether to do the actual selling yourself is entirely yours, it is wise to know your strengths. Unless you have similar sales experience, a broker's fee is likely worth the expense. Since you have already obtained an appraisal, you know what you can expect to receive for your business. A good broker will be able to increase your final sale enough to cover the expense. Moreover, they will do the work of finding a buyer, showing and negotiating, and preparing all the documents necessary for finalizing a sale.

Ask around within your food truck network to see if anyone can refer you to a broker they have dealt with before. You might also consult with your legal or financial advisors. If you seem to be out of options in the United States, you can use the chamber of commerce for your locality to identify registered brokers.

You may get a lower broker fee by working through an online marketplace, though it is standard to expect a broker to charge between 2% and 10% of the total sale price. Some brokers work for a flat fee, which may be worth considering, too. Several online marketplaces allow you to post your listing for a fee and opt to renew it every month. If you are reasonably confident in the current market activity through the site, this is a great option to consider since it eliminates the need to factor in the broker percentage.

Food truck organizations with online marketplaces where you can quickly list your truck include Food Truck Empire, Roaming Hunger, and Used Vending, to name just a few. This is an ideal option when you need to complete your sale quickly, and your total price falls somewhere in the mid or low range of the current listings. One of the benefits to selling through an online site is the increased number of people who will have access to the details of your food truck without needing to meet with each one, enabling you to weed out the less serious sellers. It also expands your range beyond your immediate geographical area. Usually, you will need to create an account with these sites, and they will perform some basic verification, though generally connecting your banking account and allowing the website to mediate the actual sale is enough insurance for them.

If your food truck is estimated to be worth considerably more than the average; if, for example, you performed extensive aftermarket improvements and purchased all your equipment and truck new, you may consider working with a broker who can identify and cultivate potential buyers with the interest and ability to match your selling price.

If you end up deciding to use a broker, even with someone else driving the selling bus, you will need to be an active passenger. After all, you know your business best and, as the owner, will always be the one most invested in the sales process. More than likely, your individual broker or company will find potential buyers by posting your listing online, too, but you will need to maintain active communication regarding when and how they will be shown the food truck. This is the area where a broker can provide benefit, too, in coordinating with potential buyers you may not have the time to.

There are many platforms dedicated to food truck sale and resale online, and your food truck network will likely be able to point you toward platforms where they have had success in the past. There are also plenty of open forums online where you can seek out tips from people who have gone through the process before. It is a wise idea to put your best foot forward with the pictures you use when posting your listing. In fact, the sales histories of online food truck sales and resale sites suggest that the more photos you provide, the faster your truck will sell.

Remember where you stood as a buyer when you were first looking into all your options and figuring out which truck best met your unique demands. Rather than avoiding showing images that reveal some of your truck's inevitable deficiencies, remember that you have accounted for all these elements when calculating its value. Your potential buyers want to have as much information as possible about what they are getting. You are more likely to have serious offers if you are upfront with the details of your truck in your listing. We wish you much luck with the sales process and hope that this chapter has given you a basic understanding of the process, easing the inevitable stress as much as possible and setting you up for success.

Chapter 14: Other Resources

Starting any small business is a huge undertaking, and we want you to have as much support as possible. In this chapter, we will cover some resources available to you as a food truck owner, everything from sales data analysis software to the various organizations that bind the food truck community together. As a mobile vendor, it can be difficult to make and maintain business connections, but the food truck industry is actively growing, and the internet is proving to be an invaluable resource in keeping food truck owners connected while driving the industry forward.

Technology is contributing more than just connectivity between those working within the industry, however. Online and mobile phone applications are equipping customers to track food trucks and access updated information, while social media have provided food trucks with a means of reaching and interacting with customers beyond those who simply happen to pass by on the sidewalk. In fact, technological advances have touched every aspect of food truck operation. Registers, for example, are hardly recognizable as the oversize, clunky machines of only ten years ago. Advances in POS systems and access to GPS technology, even digitalization of permit and licensing processes, have simplified or streamlined many of the challenges involved in establishing a successful food truck.

As established in the chapter discussing marketing, modern food trucks receive a significant percentage of their sales as a direct result of digital technologies and online marketing campaign strategies. Even financing has been impacted; crowdfunding was not even a financing option available to small businesses until recently. But many of these benefits have already been established in the previous chapters. Here, we want to take a closer look at some of the specific technologies we have yet to address and investigate exactly how you can make the most of the internet in connecting and communicating with the people in what is now your business industry, as well as accessing resources in the physical world, such as conferences specific to food trucks that can give you access to the latest information and help you stay a step ahead of the competition.

Having sung the praises of the internet, however, we want to be clear that its greatest value to you is not anything contained within the technology but in its facilitation of human connection. Your fellow food truck industry workers are the ones with the knowledge and expertise, creativity and passion, that will continue to drive this industry forward. They are the ones who will provide you with the most practical solutions and community that you will absolutely need to achieve and maintain success as a food truck business owner. Before long, you will discover that you are part of this network and actively contributing to other new food truck owners' success as they set out to provide the best possible mobile food service.

Data Analytics and Predictions

The subject of data analysis can seem dense and complicated, and we want to keep this section from falling into that trap as much as possible. As a food truck owner, you will want to save money by doing as much of the work of establishing and growing your business as possible yourself. One of the areas where this can have a significant impact is in how you address data. Your reaction, understandably, is probably a certain amount of confusion. After all, you are not establishing an IT (Information Technology) business or career, and you will be working directly with people and products every day. However, this does not make the information about that work and those interactions impossible to quantify—quite the opposite. In fact, the better able you are to collect data about your sales, ordering, finances, and customers, the more you can apply this information toward improving those statistics. While your exact situation will be unique—since no one sells exactly the food you sell, where you sell it, with equipment purchased and modified with loans from your local bank, to your set of customers—data analysis software is not specific to a situation. There are programs that will match your situation better or be a better value for your business than others.

We also want to inform you of some of the many options available to you as you work to improve your business so that you can make the most of your efforts by applying them with directed strategies informed by collected data. In general, of course, the more data you can collect, the more accurate and informative your results will be. So, what kind of business data are we talking about?

Location Data

The food truck industry is rapidly becoming as established as any other food service or hospitality industry, which comes with new regulations and the need for more advanced marketing strategies, which results in new efforts to collect and analyze data on a larger scale. You may have heard of "big data," a term referring to the collection of large quantities of information that can be analyzed by digital programs that will reveal trends, patterns, and associations. Essentially, it is a way to understand human behavior and decision-making on a grand scale.

Because of the growth and increasing digitalization of the food truck industry, companies dedicated to data collection and analysis, known as intelligence firms, have begun to collect various sets of data and perform analyses that reveal how you and other food truck owners can maximize your profit based on your location. Companies like CARTO will pick an area or group of locations that enable them to factor in how moving across city or borough limits can cost a food truck valuable time and revenue. The quicker a truck can determine the optimal location to set up, the faster they can begin to pull in sales, and the more they will minimize their daily expenses.

Analyzing location-based sales data enables these companies to create projection models. They use current sales data but also draw on many other informational sources, including the national census and foot traffic statistics. The projection models that result give you the best sense of how to make the most of your time by strategically picking your location. They also give you a much more accurate idea of what your expected sales will be at each location that can tighten your ordering and inventory, minimizing food waste.

CARTO specifically performed one of the earliest and best-known analyses of the greater New York City area in 2018. More recently, CARTO has been using special data science to investigate and help food trucks improve their sales. Their studies have determined that the most important factors in projecting revenue for a food truck are foot traffic, the amount of time between transactions, and the day of the week. It might surprise you to know that the population of the area and average rent have little impact on sales. Within New York City, locations with lower rent averages and less dense populations generated around $1,000 more in daily revenue when there were identical levels of foot traffic, for example. Traditional wisdom might suggest that you find the areas with the most people and those with the extra income they can afford to spend, but the data says otherwise, which is exactly what makes these types of studies so important. It is also a reminder that you, as a food truck owner, need to remain aware of the most up-to-date research about your industry and your specific area.

Location data has only recently begun to be factored into existing projection models since the technology has begun to allow for accurate tracking of specific locations and times of the day. Of course, just because this information is out there does not necessarily mean that food truck owners have access to it. Data models must often be purchased from intelligence companies, and food truck business owners are either unaware of this option or unable to afford it. There are, however, many studies published online for free. The only barrier you and your food truck face in accessing and adopting the recommended strategies is in knowing that they are there, which is where we come in. Following food truck forums and publications like Street Fight can help keep you up to date with the current research and advances in your industry.

It is worth considering subscribing to online food truck publications and those specific to your area, as well as creating internet alerts that will inform you any time your food truck or local area food trucks are mentioned. Some blogs you might consider following include Feedspot, Food Truck Empire, strEATs.com, and Custom Concessions, though there are hundreds more and many based out of specific cities. Remember, the food truck industry is still growing, so expect there to be some significant changes even in the next decade. You want to remain aware of—even anticipate—these new developments.

When planning where to set up your food truck each day, you do not have to guess. There is enough research now to create a data-based strategy that can optimize your location for revenue. Even if there are no studies specific to your city, the analyses from other places are still applicable. Human behavior is similar no matter where those humans happen to be behaving. Trends in similarly sized cities will likely be applicable to your city, so take advantage of the available case studies and industry research through companies like IBISWorld and SBDCNet.

Market Data and Trends

Industry market research is a great way to learn about your customers and the other food trucks you will be competing with for those customers. These studies will give you insight based on statistical data that reveals what the current demands of your potential customers are. This is another method to consider when developing your own menu, particularly if you are new to the area where you plan to establish your truck because it can help you determine whether your food truck concept is viable even before you make any purchases.

In the United States, you can access the most reliable market research through resources maintained by the federal government, which collects massive quantities of information about various industries. Specifically, you can look for the economic conditions that might suggest your food truck will be successful, information about hiring and employment that will be valuable to you as an employer, and overall industry data, including income information that is gathered from taxes.

As we suggested early in this book, there are many other organizations and companies that perform market research, either in a non-profit capacity or as a paid product. That said, there are plenty of organizations that request and conduct their own market research and surveys that are relevant to you and which you may have access to. Consider looking into local associations of mobile vendors, food truck trade groups, and business and industry publications or periodicals for research published online. Even restaurants and culinary schools will sometimes make this information available to the public.

The U.S. Small Business Administration is a fantastic resource when you are interested in performing market research and analyzing your competitors. They provide free access to information and trends involving small businesses, with lists breaking down the different forms of information and what you can get out of them. The SBA.gov Business Guide page provides links to consumer credit and product data, census and labor statistics, business and industry statistics, economic information, earnings and employment information, loan and interest data, consumer spending, and trade and market performance trends. The North American Industry Classification System website will be one of your best resources since it collects and provides statistical data intended for use in the analysis of the business economy in North America. If you cannot spare the time or are otherwise unable to conduct your own market research, however, companies like Mobile Cuisine can help facilitate research into your specific targeted market, too.

Social Media Analytics

We have discussed the importance of social media in developing effective marketing strategies, but the potential of social media extends beyond this. As a business owner, you can, in fact, use baked-in analytics in certain social media platforms to generate valuable information about the people who choose to follow your food truck online and spread information about it. We will use Twitter Analytics as an example. Like all social media, Twitter is a tool and can be used most effectively as a paid service. If you choose to, you can pay and be verified as an Advertiser on Twitter, which gives you access to analytics data about your business on the platform.

You can choose to promote specific tweets or start a campaign through Twitter, which creates graphs on your account dashboard that give you details about how your posts are being received and whether or not they are generating the kind of sharing, or retweets, that make your presence on the platform worthwhile. During any kind of financial campaign, this real-time data is even more important. For example, showing daily and monthly statistics and patterns that help you optimize your marketing strategy by determining the best methods for increasing and impacting your followers online. Twitter Analytics is particularly useful in determining whether a promotional tactic is, in fact, as effective as you believed it to be or whether you need to alter your approach.

Of course, Twitter is not the only social media platform that provides access to analytical data, so you will need to determine what makes the most sense for you. This means focusing on investing in a specific social media site or spreading brand awareness across multiple channels platforms. As you can tell, even with access to analytics, it takes time and a certain level of experience or skill to interpret this information. Here, a dedicated social media manager can be a valuable asset to your food truck business since they will be able to dedicate the time required to perform or collect effective market research that can dramatically impact your food truck's success.

Professional Resources

Membership Organizations

Within the United States, the most important food truck industry organization is the National Food Truck Association or NFTA. You can access their website at www.nationalfoodtrucks.org. The NFTA has a program that verifies and tracks member food trucks for eligibility as preferred vendors. This program is essentially a paid partnership, exchanging resources and promotional services. It is also a means for leading and established food truck businesses to connect with newer food trucks or coordinate group food service at events. Through NFTA, customers can hire catering from member trucks for private events. Businesses can even pay to have their locations added to a route list in some cities so that a rotation of different trucks will be available there on any given day. The NFTA is an excellent resource for starting a local or regional association or learning more about how larger food truck businesses operate on a national scale. For clients, the NFTA connects demand with supply, even offering businesses the opportunity to partner with trucks for advertising and promotional purposes.

They offer a wealth of resources for new trucks, too, including marketing and social media management, consulting opportunities, even tutorials to help you stay ahead of health department regulations. For startup food trucks, some of the most valuable resources include access to high-end branding photography and lists of local resources. Even if you are not yet eligible for membership, you can follow the NFTA blog, which highlights all sorts of advances, ingenuity, and opportunities within the food truck community. The NFTA is also equipped to advocate for food truck business owners at a national level. For instance, they have been able to offer financial assistance and other resources to food trucks impacted by COVID-19.

There are hundreds of regional and city-specific associations, too, and the best way to access these is through simple internet searches and talking to your fellow food truck enthusiasts, either online or in person. Specific forums we recommend include the Food Truckr podcast, Food Truck Fatty (which features a different truck every month), and the Mobile Cuisine trade magazine. There is, you have likely noticed, no trade school dedicated to food trucks or offering a degree in mobile vending, or so you thought. The Street Food Institute offers training and experience working in fully operational food trucks, awarding a certificate of completion upon finishing the program. For anyone who is hesitant about the practical and business aspects of food truck ownership and operation, this course is worth considering. Udemy also offers an online course aimed at anyone wanting to start their own food truck business.

Trade Shows and Conferences

Unsurprising for a group of people dedicated to mobility, there are hundreds of food truck trade shows, conventions, summits, expos, and conferences you can participate in within the United States every year. The chances are that you will not even need to travel far to attend at least one of the major shows, which run coast to coast. In other countries, the numbers vary slightly, but places like Canada and Australia have a booming food truck culture and plenty of access to events where food truck owners like you can share the latest news and ideas to help keep every truck successful. The prime locations for these shows within the United States include New York, NY, Santa Monica, CA, Chicago, IL, and Miami, FL.

If you are able, seriously consider attending any events with relevance to your business. Obviously, attending some of these major shows may be a major financial commitment, in which case you may choose a single larger event for the year. However, the odds are good that you are close enough to several smaller events to attend and get a sense of all the opportunities available. These shows, in addition to all their other practical benefits and exposure to cutting-edge technologies and expert speakers, can help reshape your understanding and take ownership of your industry. They run the gamut from niche (there is a tree nut convention) to general and from regional to worldwide.

These are your peers now, and these massive shows will expand your conception of what is possible for your food truck business. As with permit applications, we advise you to get your registration to your preferred shows completed early! To give you a place to start, the best known and highest attended industry shows of 2022 include:

- America's Food and Beverage Show
- American Food Innovate Summit
- Beverage Digest Future Smarts
- BevNET Live (runs an annual Summer and Winter conference, as do many of the major shows)
- Consumer Discovery Show (East and West)
- Fancy Food Show (Summer and Winter)
- Food Automation and Manufacturing Conference and Expo
- Food Safety Summit

- Food Shippers of America's Logistics Conferences
- Food and Nutrition Conference and Expo (FNCE)
- Food Processing Expo
- Food Marketing Institute's Annual Business Conference (ABC)
- Grocerytalk (Grocery and CPG event)
- International Dairy-Deli-Bakery Association Show
- International Production and Processing Expo
- IFDA Distribution Solutions Conference
- International Baking Industry Exposition
- Institute of Food Technologies Meeting and Food Expo (IFT)
- International Restaurant and Food service Show
- International Pizza Expo (Yes, this is really a thing, and anyone can attend!)
- Midwest Food service Expo
- Mid-America Restaurant Expo
- National Association of Concessions Show (NACS)
- Natural Products Expo (East and West)
- NAFEM Show (a product and equipment manufacturer event)
- National Frozen and Refrigerated Foods Convention (NFRA)
- National Restaurant Association Show
- NAMA Show (convenience service event)
- Northwest Food and Beverage World
- NOSH Live (Summer and Winter)
- Peanut and Tree Nut Processors Association Convention and Trade Show (PTNPA)
- Plant-Based World
- PLMA's Private Label Trade Show
- PMA Fresh Summit Convention and Expo
- ProFood Tech
- Refrigerated Foods Association Exhibition and Conference
- Seafood Expo North America
- Specialty Food Business Summit
- SNAXPO (snack industry event)
- SmartFood Expo
- SupplySide (East and West)
- Sweets and Snacks
- Sustainable Foods Summit
- United Fresh Convention
- Western Candy Conference
- World Tea Expo

Chapter 15: Success Stories

For some extra inspiration, we thought we would share with you just a small sampling of the many successful food trucks currently operating around the world. We have tried to provide a diverse sampling of cuisines and food service approaches to help stimulate your creativity as you put together your food truck concept. Most of these food truck business owners started just the way you are starting now: with a simple idea that you know is pure gold, one you cannot wait to share with people. If the rest of this book has equipped you with the tools and preparation to begin your business, we hope this final chapter reminds you of why you are committing to all this time and hard work and that you are infected with the passion of these fellow food truck enthusiasts.

Bacon Bacon

The concept is simple, and that is why it works. This San Francisco, CA, food truck's menu, consists entirely of bacon-based foods, including sweet dessert options. Of course, focusing a truck on a single, easily identifiable food also makes it easier to align the branding: this bacon-centric truck is hot pink.

The Bacon Truck

This Boston, MA, truck began as a brick-and-mortar location before taking its bacon on the road. We promised to provide you with a diverse sampling of trucks, so you may be wondering why we have included another bacon truck. Essentially, we want to point out that you will not have—and need not have—exclusivity over a specific food. Rather, you only need to match a demand within your target market. Both of these bacon food trucks are riotously popular in their respective cities, and each owns its cuisine in its own way. So what is our point? Basically, you do not need to offer some entirely original food or concept to run a successful food truck.

Barkery

As an example of just how extreme an idea for a successful food truck can be, this food truck sells exclusively to canine customers. Based out of Seattle, WA, this extremely successful truck found a previously untapped market: dogs. After all, they go for walks on the street every day. We simply want to make the point that, as much as we can provide guidelines for what food truck concepts have proven successful in the past, you should not be hesitant to go extreme. Branching into entirely uncharted territory is a great way to guarantee you will have an entire market to yourself.

Bernie's Burger Bus

It's not complicated. It's a big school bus that sells you big burgers and loaded fries. Customers were excited by the novelty of ordering their childhood favorites out of this repurposed bus in Houston, TX. In fact, this first truck became so popular that the business expanded into trucks in other states and even brick-and-mortar locations.

After all, childhood and burgers are not exclusive to Texas. However, during the COVID-19 pandemic in 2020, the food truck chain's owners opted not to take a relief loan and the business folded.

The Blaxican Food Truck

Founder Will Turner took his own heritage and passion for the foods of his childhood to create this dynamic mashup of soul and Mexican foods based out of Atlanta, GA. As part of this truck's commitment to supporting its community, it collects donations for Atlanta shelters as it moves throughout the city. It is clear that this food truck owner's passion is what drives every aspect of his business and has made this truck one of the most successful in the United States. An active social media presence also enables customers to track the truck across the city every day and keep them up-to-date on the charitable projects or and organizational efforts supported by this food truck. This is truly a community food truck.

The Bubble Tap

Don't forget about beverages. In this case, don't forget about the bubbly. This converted vintage trailer operates as a wine and Prosecco bar that customers can book to cater for private events. By design, this food truck (or rather, beverage trailer) operates on a different business model and work schedule than many food trucks but is all the more successful for it. By scheduling events in advance, this truck can make precise orders and ensure that no time or wine is wasted. Of course, this truck also knows its customers. Of all places to operate, New Orleans, LA, enjoys its celebrations sparkling.

Burmese Bites

New York City is a food truck bonanza. However, this means it is, if anything, harder to maintain a successful food truck within city limits. One way, proven by this truck, is to offer a cuisine no other mobile food vendor is offering. Most New Yorkers would likely have no idea what Burmese cuisine even entailed, but Burmese Bites encourages them to branch out and try something new. This truck leverages this characteristic of New York City culture of "trying something new" to great effect. Know your neighborhood!

Cinnamon Snail

This vegan truck has mass appeal because it does not aim to appeal to only vegan customers but to everyone in the greater New York City region. In fact, the story its owner tells is of wanting to serve food appealing enough that everyone wants to try it. This truck makes the most of its open hours by setting up at various farmer's markets and has expanded into brick-and-mortar locations. The Cinnamon Snail, forgive us the pun, is making its own trail through the densely populated NYC region. In this case, knowing that an area will hold a particular appeal for a larger subset of the population is a smart move. Knowing the culture of an area can give you insight into whether your truck will appeal to customers who might not otherwise consider your type of cuisine.

Curry Up Now

This food truck is a great example of how you can make the most of market momentum. Akash Kapoor found several partners to join him in 2009 to start a truck inspired by North Indian cuisine, just as the food truck movement took off in San Francisco, CA. The food is fantastic, but timing is everything, and this food truck business was able to grow from a single truck into a franchise due primarily to this timing. It is important to remain in contact with your food truck community for more than everyday support; the latest industry news can give you an edge in making lucrative business decisions. Weigh the risk, but consider the potential benefits, too!

Del Popolo

One of the best-known trucks right now is based in San Francisco, CA, and has generated buzz primarily because of its creative vehicle. The food truck is actually a converted shipping container. One wall has been replaced by glass, allowing customers to get up close and personal to the action, watching the employees prepare and cook personal pizzas in a wood-burning oven. The truck has branded itself in a way that matches this literal visibility by sourcing from Italian farming families. This truck is proof that every food truck "rule" is flexible. These gourmet pizzas average $15, nearly triple the average food truck meal cost, and that is before you add your wine selection.

The Duck Truck

The owner partners of this truck will be the first to say that no one else was offering duck in Montreal. They filled that niche, and it paid off. Take notes!

Emerson Fry Bread

Based in Phoenix, AZ, this truck melds two cuisines to great effect: Native American and Mexican. This food truck, in particular, calls attention to the ways in which traditional cuisines can be combined to create something new that catches customers' attention. Again, this truck is successful in part because the Arizona area it serves is familiar with each of these cuisines separately and is inherently curious about what a mashup might produce.

Empanada Guy

This food truck took a simple cuisine idea and succeeded by meeting demand and keeping it simple. What began as one truck in New Jersey has become ten, all serving the greater New York City area. Empanadas are versatile, able to be prepared with a variety of standard (chicken and beef) and unique (lobster) fillings. Because this food can be prepared out of relatively few ingredients, it can be served quickly and inexpensively, cutting down on the average order time and maximizing the number of orders that can be filled in a given day. The owner, Carlos Serrano, is clearly passionate about his product and travels between his trucks to meet with customers, a fact effectively promoted by his website and social media presence.

Fava Pot

This is a perfect example of a food truck focusing on regional cuisine and doing it well. Located in Falls Church, VA, this food truck offers a full menu of Egyptian cuisine. Additionally, a portion of profits from every meal purchase is donated to support female orphans in Egypt pursue education. Win-win.

Fire Truck Crepes

It's all in the name, a name that prompts you to wonder about the history of this Denver, CO, food truck. In fact, it began as a simple idea tossed around between two emergency first responders and grew into a successful business. Because of its size, the truck offers a larger menu, everything from sweet to savory crepes. But it is the story and the truck itself that grab ahold of a customer's attention. This story is shared effectively through the truck's website and social media. It is even printed on the side of the food-serving fire truck.

Gourdough's Donuts

Like many successful trucks, the name is a clever description of the food truck itself. This truck operating in Austin, TX, is not, as you might assume, a dessert truck. Each oversize donut is the foundation for a full meal. By taking an existing and already popular menu item and giving it a distinctive twist, this food truck sets itself apart from its competitors. It helps that you can personalize your donut by varying the toppings, something many trucks avoid since it tends to take longer to prepare each order. However, when you are starting with a relatively simple base food, you can afford to spend that extra time on preparation. This is a good lesson in identifying how to balance the demands of time and quality with ingenuity.

Guerrilla Tacos

This is an instance of a simple concept—tacos—melded with the culture of Los Angeles, CA, to become much more than that. These deluxe tacos are inspired by the meals many local Los Angeles residents remember from their childhood, and this keeps them coming back. The importance of understanding and embracing your food truck area community cannot be understated.

The Halal Guys

Nearly everyone in New York City knows the Halal Guys, and that is not an exaggeration. Okay, while that might be an exaggeration, what began as a simple food truck rapidly escalated into a massively popular chain. Why? Well, this food is not complicated, and it is delicious. These offerings are also what people who work late night shifts are looking for: comfort food, a reminder of home, or simply something filling to get them through the rest of the night. By selecting locations where they could operate 24 hours a day, the Halal Guys food truck all but guaranteed their success.

Heisser Hobel

Where other regional cuisine food trucks succeed because the food is offered in an area unfamiliar with it, this truck is a massive success in Berlin, Germany, precisely because its Kaesespaetzle is native to the region and is a genuine local favorite. This is where knowing your customers truly matters. How often would you patronize a local food truck that sold your favorite comfort food? Speaking for ourselves, every day.

Homegrown Smoker

Vegan BBQ. What other hook do you need? This truck uses various plant-based proteins and ingredients to allow everyone to enjoy the smoky joy of BBQ. In fact, this is the owner's reason for starting the truck. BBQ was something Jeff Ridabock did not want to lose as a vegan. By developing his own food truck in Portland, OR, he did not have to. By identifying a market demand in Portland, this food truck successfully offers a niche product that might not prove as successful in other areas.

I Don't Give a Fork

This truck began as a college competition, but founder Leigh Ann Tona created a truck that became a massive hit. In part, this is because the Delaware music scene was missing a finger-food truck and in part because of the research that went into it. Winning the competition was a bonus, but for this food truck, what mattered was finding an unfilled demand and working to fulfill it. Of course, it hurts nothing that the origin story and name catch customers' attention and pull them in.

King of Pops

In Atlanta, GA, the summers are sweltering, and ice cream trucks roam the streets. Yet this truck stands out. It offers frozen pops that are a classier, more delicious version of the ice-pops we enjoyed as kids: avocado, Mexican chocolate, tangerine basil, or cereal milk pops, for example. Like any quality establishment, the menu identifies allergens like gluten and dairy. On their website, customers can even trace the origins of all the ingredients in their pops, each locally sourced. This food truck brings together some of the most strategic approaches to success in this industry, presenting a unique twist on a single, classic food as an alternative to a market saturated by other trucks so similar that they all seem to blend together.

The Kitchen of the Unwanted Animal

Though many of these trucks are based in the United States, other countries have equally thriving food truck culture. This Amsterdam-based truck, for example, takes an unusual approach to sustainability by sourcing its ingredients from overpopulated animal species like pigeons and crawfish.

Kogi BBQ

In Los Angeles, CA, there are several trucks (and their creators) that hold a place in industry history. Roy Choi started this food truck before there was a food truck scene in L.A. It did not take long for his Korean-Mexican fusion foods to gain traction. Sometimes, it is simply worth taking notes from the experts or originals who figured out how to make the most of a moment and a hole in food culture. When this food truck opened, the hottest restaurants had just started offering Korean BBQ-inspired dishes. From within the industry, you will begin to observe these gaps and, ideally, be prepared to fill them.

Mac Mart Cart

You can't go wrong with comfort food. This food truck offers macaroni and cheese versions of classic dishes (think Buffalo chicken cheesesteak) for both meat-eaters and vegetarians. As a nod to Philadelphia, PA, food culture, each dish can be served in a bowl, sandwiched between either toast or hash browns, or poured over French fries or a hot dog. By choosing a single base and adding a variety of tasty ingredients to form each menu item, this truck is able to keep costs low and prepare dishes quickly, which keeps it operating with an impressive profit margin.

Mama Rocks

This truck is considered a Nairobi favorite now, but only because of the commitment of its founders in a region initially hostile to food trucks. The city founders anticipated change, however, and this burger truck that celebrates African flavors is a huge hit with the emerging youth culture in Nairobi. As in any industry, if you can anticipate trends, by all means, act on your insight!

Maximus/Minimus

What makes this sandwich food truck unique are the options suggested by its name. Seattle, WA, customers can choose between hot and mild options in every part of their order, food, sides, and beverages. Empowering customers to select their preferred strength and type of flavors sets this truck apart and keeps customers coming back; after all, at this food truck, they can get their pulled pork sandwich spiced just as they want.

Ms. Cheesious

The cartoon character that adorns the side of this food truck lives up to her name. This directed branding strategy paired with a variety of gourmet grilled cheese sandwiches (they even serve grilled dessert sandwiches) is a recipe for success. This truck is instantly recognizable, by sight and by name, in its home in Miami, FL. What might otherwise be an unremarkable truck is made notable by its characterization of Ms. Cheesious and the slightly unusual form in which this cheese appears. After all, how often have you had a grilled cheese outside of your own home?

Off the Rez

There is something to be said for being the first. Based out of Seattle, WA, this food truck's claim to industry fame is to be the first food truck to ever serve Native American cuisine, including frybread in all sorts of delicious forms.

Oink & Moo BBQ

Having a smoker inside your food truck is not a completely original concept, but this hardly matters when you are the first truck in the area to offer custom smoked meats. This truck was so successful in New Jersey and Philadelphia that it even opened a brick-and-mortar location. Here, again, being ahead of the game is what gave this smoked meat truck an edge over the competition. We have said it before, but do your research! Find out if there are popular trucks offering particular foods to other areas that might translate well into your region. Location, location, location.

Pierogi Wagon

Chicago, IL, is home to this welcoming wagon, the only food cart we know of to offer anything like it. There are few enough Polish offerings even in brick-and-mortar locations; this food truck brings these tasty treats to customers when they crave them the most. That is, late operating hours ensure that this truck can capitalize on the customers who are looking for the perfect food to carry them from one bar to the next.

Quiero Arepas

This Denver, CO, truck emphasizes environmental responsibility in every aspect of its business operations, something that appeals in particular to its target customer base. There are no disposable dishes, utensils, or straws to be seen. Basically, the goal of this truck is to offer Venezuelan cuisine with zero waste, and they achieve it. Moreover, effective marketing strategies ensure that their potential customers know it, too, and know where to find this truck when they are feeling puckish and eco-friendly.

Rebel Melt

Some of the most profitable food trucks are so because they are able to offer an unfamiliar regional cuisine to an area, and this truck is a prime example. This truck brings the grilled sandwich comfort food of the American South all over Canada. Taking the Rebel Melt as a case in point, food that is old news in one area may be novel in another. Remember to consider context!

The Silver Seed

This vegan food truck has found its niche within the market, catering to customers who have few (if any) options for street food in Fort Collins, CO. They market their sustainable sourcing of all their ingredients effectively, too. This truck also sets an excellent example of effective use of social media by posting their current and upcoming locations, all the more important for a truck sought out by a specific subset of food truck customers.

Snowday

Though the name may not immediately connect with a single food or image, as anyone who has experienced it knows, this food truck is all about maple syrup and social justice. In fact, rather than an individual or partnership, this truck is run by an organization: Drive Change in New York City. All menu ingredients are sourced from New York state, and the truck provides job training and employment to youth who have experienced incarceration, in many cases enabling them to return to school. The food may be delicious in its own right; however, it is this core connection to positive change and supporting community youth that keeps customers coming to support Snowday's cause.

Tapi Tapioca

This truck is evidence of how staying aware of regulation can dramatically impact your small business. Capitalizing on the opening of Brazil's cities to food trucks (where previously food trucks were not permitted), this truck also chose to stay true to the native food culture of Brazil rather than take the route of bringing in fast-food cuisines. These filled tapioca pancakes are not unfamiliar to residents; however, they are only readily accessible at this particular food truck. There are, after all, many ways to make your food truck offerings 'unique.'

Toasta

Like several other trucks highlighted here, this Melbourne, Australia, toasted sandwich truck owns its name. This truck pursues a central theme with its food, the toasted comfort foods that locals remember and crave. Here, again, there is a combination at work. The pairing of a can't-miss cuisine with a unique mobile vehicle was sure to pull in customers, and this truck has seen massive success since its inception in 2014.

The Tot Cart

Small and simple. This towable cart caters to events and parties in college-town Philadelphia, PA. What better than endless tater tots coated in creamy cheese at all hours? This food truck knows its niche and fills it well.

Wafels & Dinges

If you have ever lived in New York City, the odds are that you have heard of this food truck. From the unique name to the variety of waffles and toppings, this dessert truck has become an institution. How did it accomplish this? Well, for one, when this truck opened its doors, no one else was selling Liege, Belgian, and Brussels waffles on the street, and, as it turns out, people were very interested.

Woop Woop

With a food truck, even a gimmick can become a core component of your brand so long as the quality of your food holds up to the hype. This ice cream truck uses liquid nitrogen to turn your chosen ingredients into a frozen dessert right before your eyes in less than a minute. By doing this, Woop Woop becomes an experience as much as a meal...or, in this case, dessert.

YETI Dogs

This food truck is a great example of what sponsorship can do for your small business. The food this truck offers is not elaborate. It's hot dogs, bratwurst, and various other forms of sausage. But what is worth noting about this truck is how difficult it can be to start a small business like this somewhere like Anchorage, AK. By partnering with the YETI brand, this food truck was able to move from dream to reality.

You have likely noticed some strong similarities between many of these trucks. For instance, those that generate the most hype are often those with a strong visual impact, a hook that separates them from the crowd and encourages publicity with appealing photographs. Another similarity? Simplicity. Many of these trucks have built their menus around a single food prepared in creative or unexpected ways, or else taken an everyday food and given it a surprising twist. Another common thread is activism; many popular food trucks have aligned themselves with a meaningful cause. Not only do they serve customers delicious food, but they allow those customers the opportunity to give back by doing so, using food service to facilitate connecting at a deeper level.

There are coffee roasting trucks, popcorn trucks, ice cream float photography trucks, even trucks that sell boutique clothing alongside cupcakes. There is nothing wrong with classics, either. Hot dog and taco trucks can be just as successful as those with entirely original concepts, if you understand how to make your food your own, unify your brand, and meet market demand. We hope you take away from this chapter that the street is the only common denominator. Not only can you push the limits, but these thriving food trucks suggest that you should.

This list is by no means comprehensive. There are hundreds of incredibly inventive and financially successful trucks out there. We could name so many more: American Poutine, Bananarchy, Big Wave Shrimp, Black Spoon, Bombay Food Junkies, Flash Crabcake Company, Gastros, Humble Pie, The Lobos Truck, Mannino's Cannoli Express, Mother Clucker, The Prince of Venice, Roti Rolls, The Smoking Truck, Summer Street, Tacofino, and Van Leeuwen, to name only a few. We only hope that this chapter has given you a small taste of the infinite possibilities.

Conclusion

Congratulations on completing this first step toward owning your very own food truck business! We hope that these chapters have helped equip you with the tools you will need to achieve success as a mobile food vendor, no matter your location.

Throughout this book, we investigated each aspect of starting your business and building it into a success, beginning with setting yourself clear goals and developing a viable executive summary of your food truck business plan to present to potential investors and banks as you pursue financing. One of the most significant barriers to entry for starting your own business is often the paralyzing fear of taking on too much debt. We hope that we have been able to offer some clear guidance about the various resources available to you for making smart loan decisions and planning a successful repayment strategy.

Once you have obtained your funding, you will be able to begin the process of physically assembling your truck. The manufacturer and reseller information we provide, as well as directions on where to look for regional equipment options, should give you a head start on this process. As you develop your brand, you will get to express your passion and creativity, truly making your food truck your own while balancing your concept against the practical demands of a mobile vehicle and food service. Specifically, we have examined the areas of your new business where it is smartest to invest in outsourcing, as with developing a comprehensive brand, social media marketing campaigns, and bookkeeping.

Of course, the cornerstone of a successful business is sales. The strategies and digital software tools available to you in this book will give you an advantage when it comes to processing payment of orders and working with cash and credit in your business, whether with ordering, wages, or revenue. The sales chapter is intended particularly for anyone unfamiliar with running a business, as a general overview of the daily, weekly, monthly, and annual requirements of business owners in the food truck industry. We want you to be as well prepared as possible when you first open for business.

As part of discussing financial management, we have also delved into the specific loan and financing options uniquely available to food trucks and how to manage business lines of credit, credit cards, and crowdfunding campaigns. Of course, your budgetary requirements will depend on the cuisine you serve, but the elements you will need to account for in a standard food truck budget remain the same. We hope this chapter, in particular, will serve as a template as you begin to develop the necessary spreadsheets and work with the digital software that will keep you aware of your cash flow, helping you make the most of each sale and understand your chosen software's sales reports.

Even with a food truck, it is almost impossible to operate your business alone, at least not to the level of success you hope to achieve. In supporting this goal, we have covered the demands of hiring employees to work as part of your food truck team and the best ways to set that team up for success by developing a positive work culture from the start, combined with strong standards and training. For anyone who has never managed other workers, this is a great way to get a feel for what will be required of you and how to ensure that you are prepared to meet those challenges.

Of course, one of the biggest hurdles and expenses of food truck operation is the numerous permits, licenses, and certifications required before you can even serve your first meal. Being aware of these regulations and how they vary by location is vital to running a successful and profitable food truck. We believe that our detailed coverage of these regulations and requirements, will serve as an excellent resource as you register your business and begin the permit process for your business, yourself, and your new employees.

As you have read, we recommend beginning applications for various permits and loans early while you are still building your truck because without them, you waste valuable sales time, and the processing time for some areas can be weeks or even months long. Meanwhile, we have discussed how to deal with equipment suppliers in your industry and retain the value and functionality of your equipment through regularly scheduled maintenance.

The chapter on all legal matters involving your food truck business is another area where we hope we have effectively raised your awareness of the many tax requirements and opportunities available to your small business, the importance of insurance, and how to protect your brand. Even something so apparently straightforward as what kind of small business to register as can become a minefield, so we hope that the information in this book helps you navigate it with as little added stress as possible.

Naturally, the all-important menu gets its own chance in the spotlight, too. We have investigated various options available to you as you begin to develop a quality menu that will also be effective in a mobile setting. By offering evidence of tested methods and means of optimizing your sales based on the psychology of your customers. We hope to give you a solid start as you plan and hone your menu strategy. Your set menu is only part of this, however, and we have also investigated the various holiday and promotional opportunities that you and your food truck can capitalize on.

Having developed your menu, of course, you will need to source all your ingredients and supplies to bring it to life. We have described each type of supplier and the different benefits they offer. We also covered the importance of a commissary kitchen and the security and food safety consideration of day-to-day operations for a food truck to make sure you are not caught off guard with penalty fees or even theft.

Your food truck will be more successful the better you understand your brand and how to involve your truck in your community. These foundations can help define a strong brand and develop a customer base from which to expand. As we have explained, local connections are also where you will draw the most support and receive practical advice from experienced food truck owners and operators, whose tried-and-tested approaches are far superior to trial-and-error methods. All this community involvement is still possible and important while also strategically attending brand-appropriate festivals with your truck to increase your revenue and visibility. This book covers everything from festival applications and travel planning to partnering with local businesses for mutual benefit. One of your food truck's primary strengths, after all, is its mobility. It makes sense to leverage this function in a well-considered and strategic way.

While most of this book involves startup considerations, you may eventually need to consider selling your food truck business, and we want you to be just as prepared for this. We have delved into all the aspects of readying your truck and business for sale and some of the best strategies for getting the most out of your transaction. We hope this helps you weigh the benefits of working with brokers and how to put your best foot (or rather, wheel) forward.

We have also explored the newest predictive analytics available to you throughout the process of building your business and eventually, perhaps, even selling it. As the industry grows, there is more location and social media data available that can provide specific, directed insights to help you optimize your truck's performance and understand trends in the food truck industry.

Our final chapters also cover the many professional resources available to you as a part of the food truck community. They direct you to resources for finding local food truck associations and membership opportunities on a larger scale, as well. We have even provided a list of some of the biggest annual trade shows that can help you get involved in the food service industry to explore the many opportunities and cutting-edge strategies and technologies that can benefit your food truck business.

Altogether, the chapters in this book cover the demands and rewards of food truck business ownership in a way we hope prepares you to finally begin your own food truck journey. These chapters are a guide, but one that you must choose to follow. The decision is yours, and we hope to be able to support you in your endeavor. We cannot reiterate enough that the most successful food truck business owner is organized, flexible, and a skilled multitasker who is confident making decision after decision after decision as they lead and manage their food truck team.

But you do not need to worry if you are not the most organized or if your multitasking skills are not currently where you want them to be. Not only will you have plenty of time to practice developing those skills, but this book gives you the tools you need to train yourself into the habits that will prove invaluable as the owner of your food truck empire...oops, business. But, after all, you have all the tools. What's stopping you from taking your business all the way from a simple startup into a massive success?

Finally, if you enjoyed this book, please let me know your thoughts with a short review on Amazon. All that you need to do is to click the blue link next to the yellow stars that says "customer reviews." You'll then see a gray button that says "Write a customer review"—click that and you're good to go. It means a lot, thank you!

Roddie

© Copyright 2021

www.ingramcontent.com/pod-product-compliance
Lightning Source LLC
Chambersburg PA
CBHW071715210326
41597CB00017B/2495